> "You shall know the truth and
> the truth shall set you free"
> Yochanan (John) 8:32

VESSELS of FIRE

Testimonies from BEHIND BARS

GRM ISRAELI BIBLE INSTITUTE

VESSELS OF FIRE © 2024 by Dominiquae Bierman
All rights reserved. This book may not be copied or reprinted for commercial gain or profit. The use of short quotations or occasional page copying for personal or group study is permitted and encouraged. Permission will be granted upon request.

Unless otherwise identified, Scripture quotations are from the:
TREE OF LIFE BIBLE
Used by permission. All rights reserved.

On occasion, words such as Jesus, Christ, Lord, and God have been changed by the author back to their original Hebrew renderings, Yeshua, Messiah, Yah, YHVH, and ELOHIM, respectively.

Bold emphasis or underlining within quotations is the author's own.

First Printing December 2024

Paperback ISBN: 978-1-953502-99-5
E-Book ISBN: 978-1-953502-89-6
Printed in the United States of America

Kad-Esh MAP Ministries
52 Tuscan Way, Ste 202-412, St Augustine, FL 32092, USA
www.Kad-Esh.org

Published by Zion's Gospel Press
shalom@zionsgospel.com
www.ZionsGospel.com

Dedication

This book that contains precious and powerful testimonies from inmates all over the USA, is dedicated to those who are not serving time in prison. Yet you are in other kinds of "prisons", in other kinds of slavery and bondages. These honest testimonies will encourage you to take the GRM journey with us and be set free.

Holy Fire, burn bright in me,
You're my heart's desire,
Burn bright in me.

Sanctify my heart,
Sanctify my mind,
Sanctify my body to worship You,
ADONAI.

(*Holy Fire* by Dominiquae Bierman, the signature tune of the GRM Bible School)

Thanksgiving

We give thanks to Rabbi Baruch Bierman, the pioneer of the MAP Prison ministry, for his endless faith, love, and dedication to minister to our inmate students. His gift of healing the sick has brought forth many creative miracles in prisons. Today, he is a beloved spiritual father to thousands of sons and daughters behind bars.

We thank his anointed wife, Dr. Dominiquae Bierman, the founder and teacher of the GRM Bible Institute and the overseer of the MAP Prison Ministry. Her steadfast love, revolutionary teaching, and impartation of deliverance and inner healing are bringing many from the Kingdom of darkness to His marvelous light!

We thank Paulette Cowan and Esther Yonah for their in-person ministry to inmates in many facilities. They have traveled numerous hours back and forth to prisons to minister to many or few and even to one inmate. They are agents of hope and life, real angels of Messiah spreading the work of GRM far and wide. Their tireless efforts are bearing endless and eternal fruit.

We thank our faithful prison ministry administrator, Pastor Hanne Hansen, our dedicated prison ministry team, and the small army of MAP volunteers who tirelessly serve in the administration and visit the prisons, giving forward what they have received through GRM Bible Institute. They are located in many nations: the USA, Norway, Sweden, Malaysia, and the UK.

We thank the Chaplains, Wardens, Assistant Wardens, guards, and staff of each prison who have favored us, assisted, facilitated, and made this life-changing GRM Bible Institute possible in their institutions. We also thank the Securus team, who offered their Lantern platform for our courses, enabling the inmates to study on their tablets, and gave us countless hours of technical support.

Finally, for the most, we thank our Father in Heaven, *Abba Shebashamayim*, for sending His Son *Yeshua*, our Jewish Messiah, to die for us so that today, we can live and bring forth life from death.

> ...what will *their* (Jews) acceptance be but life from the dead?
>
> Romans 11:15

GRM Bible Institute Team

A Note from the Editor

Archbishop Dominiquae and Rabbi Baruch Bierman are anointed teachers who truly practice what they teach! The genuine warmth and love they exude are living examples of precisely what the Gospel made in Zion taught us to be: simple, true, and filled with the love of the Father. These testimonies are further evidence of the power of that Gospel when carried out into the mission field of this world. Through the GRM Bible Institute, many shattered lives and faiths broken by their own mistaken choices and the bad example of lawlessness in the church have been restored. The name for this anthology of testimonies, *Vessels of Fire*, is meant to reflect the results evident in the lives of those who have gone through the GRM Bible Institute to expose the false doctrines of replacement theology and anti-Torah that many prevalent church doctrines espouse. This prepares the true Bride of Messiah, who has been cleansed of all stains, to become *"echad"* (one) with her Groom. Being united to *Yeshua*, the Jewish Messiah, happens through being grafted into the Olive Tree of Israel. The broken lamp on the cover of this Anthology is also meant to reflect the beauty of that process, using as a metaphor the Japanese art form of

Kintsugi, whereby the potter restores broken vessels into works of art by repairing each crack with a resin mixed with gold. The end result is often more beautiful than the original piece. So it is with those of us who choose to fall on the stone that the builders rejected* and be remade according to His purposes!

Andrea Acker
Editor

In this book, we use only the initials of the inmates who have shared their testimonies for the sake of discretion for them and their families.

---

* See Matthew 21:42-44, Psalms 118:22-23

CONTENTS

Introduction: Our Prison Ministry — 1

Freedom from Bondage — 4
It Only Takes a Spark... — 6
Removing roadblocks — 8
I Found the Gospel of Hope — 10
Set Free from the Snare of Replacement Theology — 12
Freed from the Flames of Death — 16
From Islam to faith in Yeshua — 18
The Healing Miracle — 20
Discovering the True Messiah — 22
Removing the Scales on My Eyes — 24
Learning the True Measure of Love — 26
The Heart of Chanukah: Coming Home — 28
Following Jesus to Judaism and then back to Yeshua — 34
Free, Forgiven, and Grafted In — 38
Seeing Through the Inconsistencies of Christian Theologies — 42
Finding True Knowledge — 46
Turning Back to Truth — 50
Kneeling Before Elohim and Standing Up to Man — 52
From Roman Christ to the Jewish Messiah — 56
Uniting in Prayer — 60

Lifting of the Veil	62
Regaining Faith, Restoring Hope	66
The Power of the Tongue	70
Led by the Spirit of Truth	74
Learning to Love from the Source of Love	78
From Murderer to Messenger	80
Finding Shalom in the Olive Tree	84
Back to the Ancient Paths	88
From Brokenness to a Repairer of the Breach	90
I Found Salvation in the Only Name Possible, Yeshua	92
Finding "His Way"	96
A Cleansed Heart and Open Eyes	98
Reconciliation	102
I am Not Forgotten	104
A Plan for Shalom	108
No More Starvation	112
I am Delivered!	114
Deliverance from Darkness	116
New Life and Faith	118
Yearning for the Jewish Messiah	122
Finding The Holy Spirit	126
The Number 1	128
From Confusion to Clarity	130
Learning to Know My Father in Heaven	134
Removing the Biggest Stumbling Block	136
Where are You, God?	140
Lost in Religion, Found in Messiah	144
No Longer Emotionally Crippled	148
Anointing in the Dorm	152

My True Identity	154
From a Gang Leader to a Proud Member of the United Nations for Israel	156
The Blood of the Father God	160

End Word: Saving the World   *163*
How You Can Bless and Become Blessed
by the MAP Prison Ministry   *165*
Appendix: Our Resources   *167*

INTRODUCTION
Our Prison Ministry

Archbishop Dominiquae Bierman founded Kad-Esh MAP (Messianic, Apostolic, Prophetic) Ministries in 1991. Her husband, Rabbi Baruch Bierman, introduced our GRM Bible Institute into the prison system in 2017, when he first began visiting the UCI Maximum Security Prison in Raiford, Florida. Rabbi Baruch himself was saved in a US prison in 1980 when the Messiah appeared to him in his prison cell, completely changing his life.

Soon after Rabbi Baruch connected with the Messianic group in UCI, we started our first pioneer GRM Bible Institute class there. GRM Bible Institute, founded and taught by Rabbi Baruch's wife, Archbishop Dominiquae Bierman, restores the students step by step back to the original gospel coming from Zion, Israel, as *Yeshua* and His Jewish disciples preached it 2000 years ago.*

Soon, the testimonies of transformations behind bars began to come in, and we sought a way to establish GRM in the

---

* For more information and to enroll, visit www.grmbibleinstitute.com.

American prison system in a broader scope. We discovered the possibility of using the Securus Lantern application, a study platform available for inmates throughout Florida and several other states to study with tablets. Since then, the number of facilities and students has been speedily growing, already reaching several thousand in over 30 prisons. We have also established a deliverance program, an inner healing course, and other further study options. As the students' personal stories of salvation, healing, and deliverance kept flooding in, we decided to publish some of them. Most of our students grew up in one or another Christian denomination. Still, due to so many confusing and conflicting doctrines and teachings, they had never really known what to repent of and how to live a holy life, truly walking in the Spirit and Truth. Returning to the Jewish Roots of Faith and encountering *Yeshua*, the Jewish Messiah, has brought radical changes, including deep healing, into their lives. Now, they are living for His glory in and outside the prisons. A new, faith-filled, restored, and whole "Joshua generation"* is being formed behind bars with a vital connection to Israel and the Jewish people, practicing and experiencing the power of the Key of Abraham:**

I will bow down My knee to bless, favor, do good, and exalt those who bow down their knee to bless,

---

*   Generation that has the faith and tenacity of Joshua and Caleb, the Jews that led their people to possess the promised land (Israel). See the book of Joshua.

** For more teaching on the subject, order The Key of Abraham book available at www.ZionsGospel.com

favor, do good, and exalt You (Israel and the Jewish people). And I will decree a curse of misfortune and total destruction to those who dishonor and disrespect you by taking you lightly.

Genesis 12:3 STB

FREEDOM FROM BONDAGE

"For freedom, Messiah set us free—so stand firm, and do not be burdened by a yoke of slavery again."

— Galatians 5:1

TESTIMONY OF A.B.

This ministry has blessed me abundantly. Through Archbishop Dominiquae's and Rabbi Baruch's teachings, I have been delivered from the demonic oppression that I have been suffering since I was a child. YHVH has guided me in helping others to find the truth. Once I get released from prison, I plan to be part of this ministry to help set those who are in bondage and captivity free.

IT ONLY TAKES A SPARK...

"...let your light shine before men so they may see your good works and glorify your Father in heaven."
 — Matthew 5:16

TESTIMONY OF J.D.

There is a fire spreading here, and it has surprised me that as people learn the truth about who *Yeshua* is, they want to know more. I am glad that God is using you through me. The education you offer greatly helps to bring the truth to the people. Some have asked for proof, and because of GRM, I was able to take them to the scriptures and show them. I can boldly plant the seed of God's truth in people's minds, and He is watering those seeds. I pray that this movement toward *Yeshua* and His Father continues and that the fire for the Lord grows and burns brighter each day. May God bless and keep you always.

REMOVING ROADBLOCKS

Repent, therefore, and return—so your sins might be blotted out, 20 so times of relief might come from the presence of ADONAI and He might send *Yeshua*, the Messiah appointed for you.
— ACTS 3:19-20

TESTIMONY OF K.S.

GRM has taught me many things I did not know and it's very thought-provoking. I see things differently now and realize that I've been missing out on the whole truth. I also see that the eternal gospel is not being preached; therefore, the Messiah's return is being delayed. You are removing roadblocks with this bible study. Now that the door is open, I pray I'm worthy of entering. Thank you for letting me know that I am grafted into the family.

I FOUND THE GOSPEL OF HOPE

Then *Yeshua* said to the Judeans who had trusted Him, "If you abide in My word, then you are truly My disciples. You will know the truth, and the truth will set you free!"
— John 8:31-32

TESTIMONY OF J.V. (MALE)

I was raised as a Christian even though I am Jewish. For most of my life, I believed in Jesus as the Messiah. The problem was that I was not getting results. I went to Church, and I even got serious about God many times in my life, but it never lasted for long. I experienced tremendous guilt and shame. I lost faith in a God who was not working for me and began to really get angry with Him. I would think about Abraham, Isaac, and Jacob, and I began to pray to the God who knew these forefathers, the God of the living. It was about this time that He revealed to me that His Son's name is *Yeshua* and began to show me the many falsehoods that Christianity taught. I realized that I was covering up my sins through confession but not forsaking and really repenting. Then you came to this prison and shared a message from YHVH that brought both tears to my heart and joy to my soul. You people from GRM are my family. I am eternally in your debt for pulling me out of deception and lies and bringing me into the kingdom of light. May YHVH continue to bless and use your ministry to send forth the true gospel of hope and free many in the time that we have left here.

SET FREE FROM THE SNARE OF REPLACEMENT THEOLOGY

By His will, He brought us forth by the word of truth, so that we might be a kind of first fruits of all He created.
— Jacob(James) 1:18

TESTIMONY OF A.R. (FEMALE)

GRM Bible School has opened my eyes to the Word of God, to who I am, and to the role I play in the church. I have a new understanding of the Scriptures, based on which ones apply to me and which are just for the Israelites. Knowing that I am grafted into the Olive Tree is amazing! All the cliches about women's positions within the church are vaporized, thanks to you! I no longer feel intimidated or constrained by the old cliches. I now have a love for Israel and for the Jewish people. I keep you uplifted to our God in Heaven and constantly pray for Shalom for you all and your land. If God loves you as the apple of his eye, then I want to love you, too.

Discovering the true Hebrew names of God that *Yeshua* spoke to His Father was a pivotal moment for me. Being American, we naturally think of *Yeshua* as "American," but He is definitely Jewish! I know this seems silly, yet it is very true. Learning about the truth of the origins of the name of Jesus was a WOW moment for me; it was both devastating and overwhelming.* I even felt betrayed in a way I could not explain – I couldn't believe I had been referring to my Savior through a pagan Romanized name. I knew then that the real betrayal was on my end. Thanks to this course, I've been able to repent!

---

* To learn more about the original name of the Messiah, order Yeshua is the Name book available at www.ZionsGospel.com

The most life-changing topic in the course for me was antisemitism, the persecution and the murders of innocent Jewish people, and tying that back to the Scriptures and Biblical truths. I didn't connect these deaths back to God's word because I didn't know they were God's chosen people. Aside from what I'd heard at church as a child the few times I could attend, I didn't even know the Bible very well. Mrs. Dominiquae, I can go on and on about everything you have taught me! Learning about your people, their blessings, and their struggles has been amazing! You have been a gate to heaven for me.

I also learned the importance of obeying God's commandments, following the *Torah*, loving God with our whole hearts, and loving our neighbors as ourselves. Without the GRM Bible School, I would never have known these things. What a blessing you have been to me and everyone who reads your books and completes the course!

FREED FROM THE FLAMES OF DEATH

"I will put My *Torah* within them. Yes, I will write it on their heart."
— Jeremiah 31:32b

TESTIMONY OF J.V. (MALE)

This has been a life-saving course for me. I have been deceived, like so many others raised in replacement theology. Through your messages about the enemies of God and the Ark of the Covenant, I have come to realize that I also was an enemy of YHVH. My heart has been broken and I am so sorry for not living according to the truth. I have been selfish and angry at Yah and have blamed Him for the way my life has been difficult, regardless of my choices. I believed that I could just come to *Yeshua*, and confess my sins, and everything would be all right, but I now know that this is not true. I used the precious blood of *Yeshua* as if it were common. I received a covering, yet I did not change. I am no longer an enemy of the Most High. Nor am I a selfish, lost, and sinful man, but one who now has the Torah written in my heart. Thank you for pulling me from the flames of death and giving me *Yeshua* (Life)!

FROM ISLAM TO FAITH IN YESHUA

"If you ask Me anything in My name, I will do it."
— JOHN 14:14

TESTIMONY OF J.B. (MALE)

I must admit that reading the book, *Eradicating the Cancer of Religion*,* brought forth deep emotions. I have studied Islam for years and was a practicing Muslim on and off. Recently, I have been nothing but simply a seeker. However, having been a practicing Muslim makes it hard for me to be open-minded to many things, but I must break free from that.

I said the prayer at the end of *Eradicating the Cancer of Religion* book, calling *Yeshua* into my life out loud. I still have questions because I am the type of person who does not take half-steps; I want to be fully committed to God. You say in your book that religion is like cancer. I agree with the fact that every single religion has been brutal in pursuit of the cause of its beliefs. This book makes me want so badly to be restored, have a chance at a better life, and be an example for youth who are coming up as I have.

I pray that *Yeshua* will keep His promise: "If you ask me anything in my name, I will do it." (John 14:14)

I like how you break down the reason *Yeshua* had to be sacrificed and the reason for His miraculous birth. I think this was meant to happen to me. Maybe your establishment will be my foundation. You may have led me to be born again! I need God desperately to come into my life and save me from this terrible way of living. Thank you for this book. Shalom!

* Available at www.ZionsGospel.com

THE HEALING MIRACLE

These signs will accompany those who have believed: in My name they will cast out demons, they will speak with new tongues; 18 they will pick up serpents, and if they drink any deadly *poison*, it will not harm them; they will lay hands on the sick, and they will recover."

— MARK 16:17-18

TESTIMONY OF J.B. (MALE)

I had a crazy but confirmative experience. I've been asking Yah (God) to speak to me, to give me a sign so I know that I am on the right path, and I've been praying in *Yeshua*'s name.

In your book *Yeshua is the Name*, you said a believer can heal. So, I had this extreme pain in my neck for two days. Now may God forgive me if this is wrong, but I said to God: if you hear me and I am on the right path, I ask you to heal this pain in my neck. Then rubbing that spot, I said: In *Yeshua*'s name, I ask for this pain to go away! I rebuke this pain in *Yeshua*'s name!

I swear to you, it WORKED! I give my life to Yah; I know this is real. I pray that He stays with me and tells me how to walk in His light. I am praying for Israel. May our original doctrine be restored, in *Yeshua*'s name.

DISCOVERING THE TRUE MESSIAH

"We all, like sheep, have gone astray, each of us has turned to our own way; and ADONAI has laid on him the iniquity of us all. He was oppressed and afflicted, yet he did not open his mouth; He was led like a lamb to the slaughter, and as a sheep before its shearers is silent, so he did not open his mouth."
— Isaiah 53:6-7

TESTIMONY OF B.S. (FEMALE)

GRM Bible School has impacted my life in a very positive way by strengthening my relationship with *Yeshua*. I have learned more about the Jewish roots of the Messiah and replacement theology. I was, and still am, saddened to learn that Christian antisemitism grew from the soil of replacement theology. We cannot stand for this. As a result of replacement theology, the Jews are no longer understood by most Christians to be "the chosen people" but are now considered to be no different from any other people. We must work tirelessly to restore the Jewish identity of the Messiah before it is too late. In this world of misinformation and false Messiahs, we must focus on His Word instead of our human emotions. Only through *Yeshua* will we find salvation, and only in knowing the truth are we truly and completely free. When we trust fully in *Yeshua*, we will never lack for anything.

This course opened my eyes to His true identity. By taking this course, my spirit has grown by leaps and bounds. I have learned more about *Yeshua* this year than in my entire life. Without this class, I would still wander around like a lost sheep, trying to find my way back home.

REMOVING THE SCALES ON MY EYES

"...Laying hands on Saul, he said, "Brother Saul, the Lord—Yeshua, the One who appeared to you on the road by which you were coming—has sent me, so that you might regain your sight and be filled with the Ruach ha-Kodesh."
— ACTS 9:17

TESTIMONY OF J.P. (MALE)

While growing up, I studied the Pentecostal Apostolic teachings. Coming to prison, I studied Orthodox Judaism for about 6 years, and then after that Islam. Recently, I became a semi-practicing Muslim. Still, I was feeling lost and lonely these past few months. At first, I assumed it was the loss of my mother last March, but during Ramadan, watching infighting and arguments about how to believe and how to pray, I finally began to understand. Since I have been doing GRM, I am beginning to realize that it is not about me; it is about *Yeshua*. The loss of the traditional roots upon which He is founded can only be traced to Judaism, not Jesus or Isa, as Jesus is called in Arabic. The attributes and meanings do not add up apart from His Jewish roots. However, as I have begun to believe and understand these facts, the scales are lifting, and I am becoming happier as my knowledge of Yah is growing.

I thank all of you for this experience, and may the God of Abraham, Isaac, and Jacob - the Mighty, All-Knowing, and All-Hearing One - bless every one of the sponsors, coordinators, and volunteers at GRM!

LEARNING THE TRUE MEASURE OF LOVE

"For God so loved the world that He gave His one and only Son, that whoever believes in Him shall not perish but have eternal life."

— John 3:16

TESTIMONY OF S.Y.P. (MALE)

After studying the GRM Bible School course I have a greater desire to have Yah's *Torah* written upon my heart, which can only be done by receiving the anointing. I was so impacted when Archbishop Dominiquae shed tears of sorrow over people who do not understand what it means to love God. It finally hit home for me. All my life, I struggled to understand that very concept. I knew deep within my heart that demonstrating our love for our Father in Heaven was being obedient to His Commandments. I justified it away; I did what was right in my own eyes, and that is why I am in prison. I found our Jewish Messiah there, and through His servant Dominiquae Bierman, *Yeshua* led me to understand the true measure of love, to love YHVH, God, with all our hearts. Now I don't strive to obey God's Commandments, His *Torah*, because I 'have to,' but because I love Him and His Son *Yeshua*. Had I not been so stubborn and allowed Him to let me know His Love before, I would have been a better husband and father.

THE HEART OF CHANUKAH: COMING HOME

Then came Hanukkah; it was winter in Jerusalem. Yeshua was walking in the Temple around Solomon's Colonnade. Then the Judean leaders surrounded Him, saying, "How long will You hold us in suspense? If You are the Messiah, tell us outright!"

Yeshua answered them, "I told you, but you don't believe! The works I do in My Father's name testify concerning Me. But you don't believe, because you are not My sheep. My sheep hear My voice. I know them, and they follow Me. I give them eternal life! They will never perish, and no one will snatch them out of My hand.

— John 10:22-30

TESTIMONY OF R.W. (MALE)

On day one, as soon as they lit the first candle, I felt the Holy Spirit move in me. A volunteer stood to read the history of the menorah,* and I was transported back to the times of old. With my eyes closed, I listened and imagined what it must have been like to be there in those days. I must have dozed for a few seconds because an angel spoke to me, saying, "As it was, so it is." I turned to him and asked, "What does that mean?" He responded, "It doesn't have to mean anything; it just is, as He just is," and then I came back to the service, wide awake. I was thrilled at the message, and the rest of the service became a worship session that emanated from the very marrow of my bones.

On the second day, we had a feast. The family of another inmate donated yellow rice mixed with chicken and cheese, fried plantains, and two kinds of cake with frosting. Real tears of joy rolled down my cheeks as I savored every bite. My seat was right in front of the menorah, and I watched the flames dance and flicker as I inwardly gave thanks, praise, and worship for such a marvelous plate. Then during the reading for the second day, I felt my face begin to glow because I felt the presence of HaShem as surely as Moses did.

On the third day, I almost didn't go. I had caught a cold or flu and didn't feel well. However, as service time approached,

---

* the Jewish seven-branched candelabra

I felt an almost magnetic pull. I began to tell myself that if I were ill then I needed to be where He was. I went to service and as soon as I walked in, all my symptoms disappeared. That night, we fellowshipped, and I began to know my Messianic brothers in a way that I had not known before. The room full of men became a room full of faces, and then a room full of character and personality, and then it became a room full of family- My Family.

On the fourth day, we had a movie, "The Bad News Bears" (the new version), and we all laughed together and had potato chips and coffee.

On the fifth day, it was my turn to tell the Chanukah story, as I was the fifth candle. While I didn't 'curtsey' as the text indicated, I did give a joyful rendition. Of note, and I pointed this out to one of my brothers, is the fact that for some reason, the fifth candle on the menorah burned at least 15 minutes longer than the rest. I took it as a personal sign from *Yeshua*.

The sixth day was special. I learned the Shema and was allowed to sing it aloud. Now, it replays over and over in my head and comforts me; it's like a song that you hear over and over, and I love it!

On day seven, our pastor noted the dwindling of our number. On prior days, especially feast days, we had 120 or more (that's a lot for a prison), but on day seven, there were only 50 or so, with lots of empty seats. We had the best service anyway. We blew the shofar, sang the Shema, and fellowshipped with coffee as our brethren read the menorah story of the seventh day (and the Maccabees). Service was cut short due to miscommunication with security staff (we had to leave at 7:30 instead of 8:00), but someone asked the question, "Didn't we already accomplish our service anyway?" and we all agreed that we had.

Day eight was very special for me. Have you ever gone to an airport or train station, and as you were leaving, you felt a weird feeling in your stomach because you would miss whoever was not going with you? I felt like that the whole time. I knew I would miss the service and the menorah. I knew I would miss the closeness I had finally achieved with my Creator. I drank my coffee as if it were the last I would have. I shook hands and hugged my brothers as if I would never see them again. I sang loud, and I worshiped as if I were immersed in a pool filled with the Holy Spirit, and I felt a great loss in my chest as the last candle sputtered and died.

That's not the end of the story, however. The next day was Friday, the beginning of Shabbat. I walked from the dining hall timidly toward the service room where we usually meet. There was misty rain, so the ground was wet. I noted that no one else was walking towards the meeting room. I felt small and alone. I saw an officer looking at me (through my peripheral vision), and the uneasy knot of "I'm not supposed to be here" began to tie itself in my stomach. The door handle was wet and cold. Still, I was determined to see it through, so I reached out and pulled the door, and it easily opened! It wasn't locked! Not only was it open, but warm air washed over me from a well-lit (please note the emphasis on "light") room, and the rich smell of coffee washed over me, and a smile grew from ear to ear on my face. It felt like coming home, and I sat in a chair and cried joyfully. The pastor asked me to explain. I stood before all of my brothers and told them what I just told you. It was significant because for Chanukah, we were allowed to assemble in the compound game room, but for regular Shabbat services, we gathered in a different room on the other side of the compound.

I felt moved to share this heartwarming story of Hanukkah with you as I am resuming my studies and quizzes for GRM. Thank you for "being there," and Happy Chanukah.

FOLLOWING JESUS TO JUDAISM AND THEN BACK TO YESHUA

Sacrifice and offering You did not desire—my ears You have opened—burnt offering and sin offering You did not require. Then I said: "Here I am, I have come—in the scroll of a book it is written about me. I delight to do Your will, O my God. Yes, Your *Torah* is within my being."

— PSALMS 40:7-9

TESTIMONY OF A.T. (FEMALE)

The GRM Bible School was brought to my attention by a friend to enhance my Jewish knowledge, which I realized was lacking. I fell in love with the teachings from the first lesson and continued until the last lesson. I was raised Catholic but after dating my (present) husband who was Jewish, I decided to convert to Judaism before we were married. We followed the traditional conservative practice of Judaism for the last 35 years, as until taking this course I didn't realize I had an option to be both Christian and Jewish. I always felt a yearning to practice both and now because of the GRM Bible School, I have a much deeper understanding of what Messianic means. I now feel whole and am in a better position to mentor my husband's family and my sons on the relationship between the Old and New Covenant. The prophecies of the coming of the Jewish Messiah in the Holy Scriptures point to, beyond a shadow of a doubt, the same Messiah in the Bible of the New Testament.

Because of GRM I now have a better understanding of anti-Semitism and why events such as the Shoa (also called the Holocaust) can never be forgotten. I understand all the laws and holy days and why it is so important to follow exactly what YHVH instructed in the Commandments. Through this journey of returning to my roots, I discovered my identity. This course gave me a deeper understanding of how antisemitism through history was so prevalent, leading the way to Replacement Theology from the infamous Council of Nicaea, Constantine, to the Pogroms and the many wars against the Jewish people. It also taught me how storms and weather are YHVH's wrath and judgment upon the nations, and that only through repentance, restitution, and obedience to the Holy Scriptures, as written on the tablets of stone, will we begin to see our loving YHVH.

FREE, FORGIVEN, AND GRAFTED IN

"I am the vine, you are the branches. He who abides in Me, and I in him, bears much fruit; for without Me, you can do nothing. If anyone does not abide in Me, he is cast out as a branch and is withered; and they gather them and throw them into the fire, and they are burned. If you abide in Me, and My words abide in you, you will ask what you desire, and it shall be done for you. By this My Father is glorified, that you bear much fruit; so you will be My disciples."

— John 15:5-8

TESTIMONY OF M.M. (FEMALE)

GRM Bible School is impacting me in so many ways by helping me to separate myself from the Replacement Theology I have been taught throughout the years. In 1997, I was spiritually born-again, taught, and brought into a relationship and knowledge of *Yeshua* under the teachings of my Jewish in-laws. However, as the years progressed, I began accepting "the normalized society" pagan holidays regarding *Yeshua*'s birth, death, burial, and resurrection, even though I knew the dates were wrong and that it was celebrated incorrectly. As I began to slowly saturate myself in these theologies and doctrines, I also slowly began to observe Jewish Messianic days such as Shabbat, holidays, and feasts less and less. I did not see the importance of keeping the original timing and seasons anymore. Looking back, I realize that I was a mess and blinded by a web of lies. When I gave my life to *Yeshua* at age 18, He had already provided me with a surrounding of His people, His ways, and His Truth, but I allowed the world's systematic-regular Christian theology to replace the knowledge and faith that I had.

There was one book at my prison called, *The Identity Theft*,* that everyone was talking about (including those who are not of similar faiths/denominations/religions), so I decided to see what it was all about. I am very picky regarding what I read

---

* Available at www.ZionsGospel.com

because I have noticed that something is amiss in the Body of Christ; however, I could not place it nor did I feel I could do anything about it except to monitor what I feed myself spiritually. As I flipped through the pages of The Identity Theft, the first words that caught my attention were "the divine call to a church like Esther." I became emotional, even crying, and then I felt and saw in the Spirit that the protective walls that I had built over the years were vibrating and shaking. They didn't crumble or break down, yet they shook! I said to myself: "Oh God, this is it! This is what I have been looking for!" I finished the chapter and went back to the beginning.

I know that the GRM teachings are inspired by the Holy Spirit because these courses pierced my heart, spirit, and mind. As I am reading, listening, learning, and understanding the curriculum and assignments, a new fire is igniting inside of me and removing Replacement Theology. GRM has brought back to my remembrance the knowledge that I had forgotten and the importance of returning to the roots of my faith in the Creator whom I love and serve. I am embracing my identity, just as Esther, being of Jewish blood who became a Persian, embraced her forgotten identity as a Jew. Although I am not Jewish by blood, I have been adopted and embraced through the blood of the Jewish Messiah, *Yeshua*.

I want that restoration for my household, family, friends, and nation; to break the generational curse placed on this world through this Replacement Theology which leads to abominations against Elohim! After reading, studying, and hearing the teachings from all the assignments by Archbishop

Dominique and Rabbi Bierman, I understand that in the 4th century, Constantine and the Council of Nicaea declared a divorce of Christianity from the Jewish Roots of its original foundations on the Jewish faith, calendars, and customs. This separation caused a ripple effect for all nationalities of people to lose their salvation.

I have used this new knowledge to help me explain to others how blinded we have been. Without the GRM coursework, I only knew of some of these things but could never articulate them in words, but this course has given me boldness in sharing Yah's Word where even a baby cannot err. I truly cannot thank all the GRM staff, and especially Archbishop Dominiquae and Rabbi Bierman, enough! I am free! I am forgiven, and I am grafted into the Olive Tree! Thank You!

SEEING THROUGH THE INCONSISTENCIES OF CHRISTIAN THEOLOGIES

> All Scripture is inspired by God and useful for teaching, for reproof, for restoration, and for training in righteousness, so that the person belonging to God may be capable, fully equipped for every good deed.
> — 2 Timothy 3:16

TESTIMONY OF N.D. (MALE)

One of the most important subjects I've studied through GRM is antisemitism in the Christian church, government agencies, social groups, and nations and empires which have since fallen, as well as those still around today. I now see how I was antisemitic when I was younger, and I've had to take a deep look at myself and lift it up to *Yeshua* for forgiveness. GRM has impacted my life heavily by teaching me the true gospel of *Yeshua* and helping me understand the Torah and the books of the Prophets.

The four courses I took and the books that come with the lessons have taught me why the Torah is still in effect and how the Christian doctrine was established. It always puzzled me when I was told as a child that the Torah was no longer in effect. I asked my pastor simple questions, such as, "Why is it in the Bible then?" Through what GRM Bible School has taught me, I understand that I had been manipulated time and time again by the Catholic church, which began following the establishment of the Council of Nicaea, and by the edicts of Constantine, who at the time was the leader of the Roman Empire. Through the Council of Nicaea, they combined Sacred Holy Days with pagan holidays, henceforth creating a new religion and "bringing the people together" so that the Roman Empire would have more control over their population. They also changed *Yeshua* into a Roman Christ, and even up until today, His real identity has been lost. With this knowledge, I can now discern truth from fiction and see how the Christian masses have been led astray. I am genuinely thankful you blessed me with this opportunity.

FINDING TRUE KNOWLEDGE

I will bow down My knee to bless, favor, do good and exalt those who bow down their knee to bless, favor, do good and exalt You. And I will decree a curse of misfortune and total destruction to those who dishonor and disrespect you by taking you lightly.
— Genesis 12:3 STB

TESTIMONY OF M.C. (MALE)

I became interested in Messianic theology due to the heart and soul issues I had developed over the decades of being a run-of-the-mill Christian. I thought I knew the Gospels and what they taught, and I believed that my relationship with the Father was OK, but I was missing something. It took me coming to prison and being handed a 25-year sentence to face the facts. I was lost - I had no hope or real beliefs beyond the watered-down grace message I had accepted.

Then, one day, many years into my sentence, I had a Messianic bunkie, and we started to talk. I went to a service and have not looked back! I was there on the first night that the GRM team came to visit us. I listened to Esther and Paulette work in the Spirit and truth and immediately signed up. I have been taking my time doing this course and have learned so much. I have searched my heart and have rid myself of all antisemitism and thus become a member of the real covenant with *Yeshua*. As I am intensely studying the Torah and the Hebraic roots of His Ministry, the sick part of my spirit has begun to heal and is being filled with a true understanding of the gospels. With the help of the Archbishop's teachings, I'm experiencing a fuller and more Spirit-lead life in my worship and prayer and even in the ministerial outreach I now lead.

As a whole, GRM has made a life-changing impact on me and those around me. However, if I am asked to pick the most life-changing topic, it is *the Key of Abraham* (Genesis 12:3)*. Seeing the outcomes of so many countries and nations blessing or cursing Israel and then having the consequences of their stance toward Israel show up and manifest in different ways is astonishing. Looking back at my life and seeing the effects that have occurred in my own life is even more compelling. Understanding the Key of Abraham has unlocked a whole new depth to my gathering of knowledge and the application of it to my life.

Now, with the war against Hamas spreading, I'm seeing more and more hate and evil coming out of unexpected places. Dr. Bierman has been equipping and strengthening me to be a force for good and a light in the darkness. Praise the Lord! I'm excited to continue learning with further courses and attending GRM services, thus adding to my armor and knowledge. The Father says "My people die for lack of knowledge,"** and he also says He gives knowledge freely to those who ask of him. I am asking, and he is giving, blessed be the name of his glorious kingdom. Shalom.

---

* To learn more about this powerful key, read my book *The Key of Abraham* available at www.ZionsGospel.com.

** Hosea 4:6

TURNING BACK TO TRUTH

"You will know the truth, and the truth will set you free!"
— John 8:32

TESTIMONY OF C.C. (FEMALE)

I was raised Catholic, yet I feel that I am now hearing the truth for the first time in my life. I absolutely love this course. This is my 36th year of incarceration, and finally, I'm learning the truth – a truth that no one can ever take away from me. Thank you so much.

KNEELING BEFORE ELOHIM AND STANDING UP TO MAN

Now we know that we have come to know Him by this—if we keep His commandments. The one who says, "I have come to know Him," and does not keep His commandments is a liar, and the truth is not in him. But whoever keeps His word, in him the love of God is truly made perfect. We know that we are in Him by this—whoever claims to abide in Him must walk just as He walked.

— 1 John 2:3-6

TESTIMONY OF D.D. (MALE)

First, I would like to say I'm not good at comprehending things. I thank GRM for making this easy and enjoyable. GRM changed my perspective on how I view Christianity. GRM made me realize we're separated and that we all need to come together. Satan wants us to be divided, but it is time to rise and stand for what we believe in, even if it costs us our lives.

The church today is watered down. No one speaks the truth in the church, maybe because they don't know the truth. It's good that GRM teaches us the roots and how it began. This is a great course, and I'm continually recommending others to sign up so that they, too, can learn the truth so that the truth will set us free. It's important to be able to discern what is real and what is not. All we need to do is stick to what is written. The problem is that people think they can interpret the scriptures, but only the Holy Spirit can reveal things to us.

The topic that stood out to me the most was the Ark of The Covenant. It brought chills to me and almost made me cry. Following what was stored in the Ark, the commandments hand-written by God, was what could save the Jewish people. It's the same with the people in the church; just because they can quote scriptures that they will be saved does not mean they will be. We're so caught up with the things of the world when we should be storing our treasures in heaven where there cannot be rust*. We must be willing to leave behind the extra baggage.

I pray for restoration all the time. I want all of *Yeshua*'s people to unite and become one. The end times are near, and our people are separated because of the lack of knowledge. *Yeshua* wants us to all fully surrender and turn from our wicked ways and confess our sins, but the churches aren't preaching what the people need to hear. We need to return to the Jewish roots of faith even if people dislike us because we're not here to please man. I continue to pray for Israel and the reconciliation of the church, and that *Yeshua* will bring equipped leaders to us.

---

* See Matthew 6:20

FROM ROMAN CHRIST TO THE JEWISH MESSIAH

Do not be conformed to this world but be transformed by the renewing of your mind, so that you may discern what is the will of God—what is good and acceptable and perfect.

— Romans 12:2

TESTIMONY OF T.B. (MALE)

Through GRM Bible School, the way Archbishop Dominiquae directed me through this course to truly repent was life-changing. Growing up, I repented of some things in my life, but I never repented from treating Israel lightly or the antisemitism I was immersed in and didn't even realize! After I sincerely prayed all the prayers given throughout the courses, a weight was lifted off me, and I began to have divine peace within myself.

These classes also expose the deceptions that Satan has penetrated the churches with, through Constantine and the 4th century, and beyond. I grew up in a family that still celebrates Halloween, Christmas, and Easter. Through these course materials, I have learned what these holidays actually represent. They say in the secular world that Christmas is the happiest time of the year. Satan blinds society into believing this, yet bringing to them the highest suicide rates of any time of the year. Today, the church is not grafted into the Olive Tree but into a Roman pagan Christmas tree. The modern church has lost its true identity. Most Christians in the world don't know the true Messiah and Savior. All they know is the Romanized Christ. The fruit of communing with a Roman Christ rather than a Jewish Messiah has brought bloodshed and cruelty throughout history, which I was never taught.

Since I now know all this, I have devoted the rest of my life on this earth to not participating in any of Satan's schemes about these pagan holidays. I will only observe the LORD's commanded feasts. I will also not remain silent on these issues. I even spoke about these pagan practices to my family. Since I took this course through GRM, I now pray for Israel daily and embrace the Torah's instructions in my life. My relationship with *Yeshua* is not a religion but a relationship that I embrace, just like (the faith) in the 1st Century.

On my journey of returning to my Jewish roots of faith, I had to learn first how far away from the truth, from the first-century teachings, I had gone. I had to learn about all the deceptions that have been taught to me. When GRM taught me how far history has taken us from the Jewish Messiah, I knew I had to return to the original roots, back to the Messiah. The modern church is so corrupt, and they don't even know they are corrupt. Now, when I observe videos from modern churches, all I see is fake entertainment and everyone in the pews staying stagnant, just like Satan wants them to. Now that I have turned back to the true Messiah, I am alive and have a true purpose, a God-given calling. I need to help open others' eyes to know the same truths so they, too, can return to the first-century Messiah, just as I did.

UNITING IN PRAYER

Our battle is not against flesh and blood, and we wage Your war against Amalek with the spiritual weapons of prayer, fasting, and praise. You are fighting this battle, and we say, "Let Yahveh arise and let all Your enemies, the Amalekites, and all their friends and allies be scattered seven ways away from us, from Your bride and from Israel in Yeshua's Mighty Name!"
— **Anti-Amalek Prayer**

TESTIMONY OF L.S. (FEMALE)

Thank you so much for sharing the GRM Bible School teachings. I have been mightily blessed, and I'm only halfway through. I'm very much looking forward to soaking up more of His Word. I am sharing the prayer against Amalek* with my family, and my Momma is going to share it with her congregation, too. It is such a powerful prayer, and what an honor it is to be praying with so many to our Heavenly Father. Thank you also for all the news updates and the honest reporting from Israel. Being where I am, I do not receive accurate news without bias. You and the Ministry are in my prayers. Shalom.

* Read and download our Anti-Amalek prayer at https://kad-esh.org/prayers-for-israel/

LIFTING OF THE VEIL

But whenever someone turns to the Lord, the veil is taken away.
— 2 Corinthians 3:16

TESTIMONY OF S.P. (MALE)

The most striking impact of this course on me is that I see the workings of the Ruach HaKodesh in the lessons. These lessons have often confirmed what our kehillah has learned and discussed in our own Bible studies and given us truths we were unaware of. They are an additional witness to what I have personally learned through my schooling with the prison's Kh'rev Torah Yeshiva Messianic Jewish Seminary. The GRM Bible School has been God's gift to us to bring others into Messiah's faith, and not only that but a great tool in bringing revival into the more dormant members of our *kehila** Toda!

I have also shared the truths I have learned from Archbishop and Rabbi Bierman with my five adult children. I was not raised in a religious or faith-based home. Even my Jewish identity was hidden from me until my aunt and family revealed a little here and a little there. I never trusted anything "Christian" as I was persecuted as a preteen and teen at the private "Christian" school I was forced to attend. This course has helped me overcome my bitterness towards anything "Christian" and learn to love them as lost brothers and sisters just as I love my lost Jewish brothers and sisters. I see now that there is a veil over the eyes of Christians just as there is over the eyes of many in the Jewish communities.

---

* Hebrew word meaning *congregation*.

Lastly, I have always felt women could be spiritual leaders as well as political activists from knowing about Deborah, Hulda, Phoebe, etc. and I was always troubled by Shaul's negative instructions that contradict his other writings. The lessons in Unit 19 and the book 'The Woman Factor' really helped set the record right. Praise the Holy One of Israel!

REGAINING FAITH, RESTORING HOPE

Therefore everyone who hears these words of Mine and does them will be like a wise man who built his house on the rock.
— Matthew 7:24

TESTIMONY OF T.M. (MALE)

GRM Bible School has given me an enormous amount of information and knowledge of history that I was never aware of. It has helped me to understand Jewish culture and the Torah. As I have been following *Yeshua* and searching for a better understanding of His Word, this course has given me a better understanding of what it means to have *Yeshua* as Lord and Master of my life. The way that Archbishop Dominiquae teaches each section makes it an extremely pleasant time spent in the Word. It has changed my outlook on His Word and what it really means to be Jewish and understand the foundations of the Jewish Faith.

I have tried various churches and different types of Religions, but none could lead me to the true path of the Messiah. I tried Pentecostal, Baptist, Seventh-Day Adventist, Lutheran, and many others with no success. All this time I was walking around believing the so-called "false truth" of their teachings. Until I found and received the true Jewish Messiah, I was lost and empty. I was living without purpose, hope, or even true faith in anything from man. However, the moment I accepted *Yeshua* as my personal savior and Lord I found true life. Since I've been attending the Messianic Services and keeping the Sabbath, I have found peace, joy, new life, and real meaning in my life. I am overflowing with joy that I finally found my way home to *Yeshua*. I now understand what it means to be grafted into the Olive Tree and into another family, the family of Yah.

Through this school, I have regained my faith in *Yeshua*, and it has restored my hope for a better life, not just here on earth but also the assurance of a better life in eternity. I'm very grateful to everyone at the GRM School who has worked long hours with many sacrifices to bring these courses to people who could have been lost forever.

THE POWER OF THE TONGUE

"From the fruit of his mouth a man's stomach is filled—with the harvest of his lips he is satisfied. Death and life are in the control of the tongue. Those who indulge in it will eat its fruit."

— Proverbs 18:20-21

TESTIMONY OF T.M. (MALE)

The most powerful effect GRM Bible School has had on my life is to show me the importance of honesty and the strong influence words have on people and environments. The spirit-lead books in this course have exposed the truth to the world that has been misled for far too long because of deception and selfish needs.

The book that stood out the most was *The Healing Power of the Roots* because I experience the healing power of the roots every day of my life. My old life was governed by a mentality of "ride it till the wheels fall off." I came to the point where the only options were to submit to death or submit to God, laying in a bed with my body falling apart and my mind and thoughts in chaos. My world was falling down around me, and I knew I couldn't do it anymore. I admitted I knew nothing and that I needed a better way. GRM Bible School showed me that better way. My body started healing itself as I connected to my Jewish roots and followed the lead of the spirit toward Israel, God, and salvation. Anything else just leads us further away from Him and will always leave us confused.

I learned how important it is to always speak honestly because dishonesty can have serious consequences. When leaders turn away from God, they lead their entire nation away from God. Dishonesty disrespects the spirit and is disloyal to God. Understanding the importance of the words we choose to speak plays a huge part in the way we influence the world around us. Life and death are in the power of the tongue. The words we choose show us what our character truly is. Our words also show us how we truly feel about God, and what is in our hearts. If we speak the words of God then we should also walk in the words of God, watching them come to life. We should strive to allow God to lead our walk with His Word and to see His promises manifest so that we can witness the love and glory of the living God of Israel, the God of the universe.

Taking part in this course has verified everything the Spirit has been telling me for the past few years. I never doubted the Spirit, but until taking part in this course I was afraid to act on what the Spirit was telling me. Now I know it is time to move and to be strong in the Word of God, thus restoring the children of God to the Jewish roots of their faith, so that all nations can know God. Through the GRM Bible School, Archbishop Dominiquae and Rabbi Baruch have become a living testimony that I am not alone. I now understand that God has placed His children where we have been placed to do His work and is now bringing us all back to our motherland to enjoy His promises.

LED BY THE SPIRIT OF TRUTH

"They said to one another, "Didn't our heart burn within us while He was speaking with us on the road, while He was explaining the Scriptures to us?"
— Luke 34:32

TESTIMONY OF S.V. (MALE)

GRM Bible School has impacted my life dramatically. So much of what the Spirit revealed through GRM stirred my spirit from within just as the Bible says in the Book of Luke. As I read the materials and listened to the audio teachings, the Spirit of God bore witness to the truths that were being revealed. The Spirit brought me to a passage in Scripture found in the Book of 1 John 5:6 that says, "…And it is the Spirit that bears witness because the Spirit is truth," as well as John 16:13, "The Spirit of Truth …will guide you into all truth!" I believe that the Spirit of Truth has led me to GRM Bible school to have you "expound to me the way of truth more perfectly," as Aquila and Priscilla did for Apollos in Acts 18:26.

I have been incarcerated for over thirty years and have "given attendance to reading" (1 Timothy 4:13) and the Spirit has instructed me to "study to show (myself) approved" (2 Timothy 2:15). As the Apostle Paul wrote in the Book of Galatians, "For I neither received it of man, nor was I taught it, but by the revelation of Jesus Christ" (Galatians 1:12). The Holy Spirit has revealed these wonderful truths to me; "…the Holy Ghost teaches, comparing spiritual things with spiritual" (1 Corinthians 2:13).

So many of the confessing believers around me read books that are not the Bible, and do not do as the Bereans, "…in that they received the Word with all readiness of mind, and searched the Scriptures daily, whether those things were so" (Acts 17:11). Because they did not make a habit of going to the Holy Scriptures to confirm the truth they became "tossed to and fro with every wind of doctrine" (Ephesians 4:14). The Spirit brings another Scripture to mind that is found in the Book of Hosea 4:6, "My people are destroyed for lack of knowledge." GRM has impacted my life so profoundly because it was very discouraging to believe that I was the only one to believe the Scriptures in the way that I do, as the Prophet Elijah felt. Yet God has revealed to me, as He did to Elijah in the Book of 1 Kings 19:18, "Yet I have left seven thousand in Israel, all the knees which have not bowed unto Baal." Sister Dominiquae, you have greatly encouraged me. I am profoundly grateful because now I am encouraged that I am not alone.

LEARNING TO LOVE FROM THE SOURCE OF LOVE

"We love, because He first loved us. If anyone says, "I love God," and hates his brother, he is a liar. For the one who does not love his brother, whom he has seen, cannot love God, whom he has not seen. And this commandment we have from Him: that the one who loves God should also love his brother."

— 1 John 4:19-21

TESTIMONY OF T.B. (MALE)

Studying at GRM has truly been an enlightening experience for me. My eyes have been opened to things about both Yah and the Jewish Messiah that I never knew. It's been very rewarding, especially because I grew a little closer to my Creator through it. The books of GRM have truly been a journey of revelations. I never knew the history of Constantine[*], so that was very enlightening. Learning the true name of the Jewish Messiah was compelling. I thank GRM for giving me the great opportunity and honor of learning all I have. It's truly changing lives here at the prison. It proves that both Jew and Gentile can be brother and sister and that the Lord loves us all. We must fall head over heels in love with the Holy Spirit because if we don't, we can't love God Himself, and it's only by the love of the Holy Spirit that we can have true love for each other. The Holy Spirit gives us true love for God, His Word, and for each other. The Holy Spirit gives us strength and comfort in our times of need and teaches us truth and wisdom from above. May He bless you and keep you!

---

[*] The Eastern Roman emperor who established Christianity as the official religion of the Roman Empire through the Council of Nicaea 325 AD, based on replacement theology.

FROM MURDERER TO MESSENGER

"He told them, "Go into all the world and proclaim the Good News to every creature. He who believes and is immersed shall be saved, but he who does not believe shall be condemned."
— MARK 16:15-16

TESTIMONY OF T.B. (MALE)

This course has been a huge blessing in my spiritual walk and key to my understanding of how *Yeshua*, my Savior and Messiah, desires to be worshiped. I have been looking for "The Truth" in my walk and study of scripture for many years. About six years ago, through a precious friend, I was introduced to Messianic Judaism. My walk with our Savior changed forever! I am learning the Hebrew language and am now able to read and study the Holy Scriptures the way we were intended.

I am 63 years old and gave my life to Jesus in the Southern Baptist church I was brought up in when I was 13 years old. There I rarely heard the word "Jew" spoken. When it was spoken it was generally used negatively. I thus lived most of my 63 years knowing about antisemitism and its effect on the Jewish people, yet I had no idea where all the hatred originated. I did know that many considered them the 'murderers of Christ'. As I entered my later teenage years, I discovered the joys of the female sex and fell prey to drug and alcohol abuse. My walk with the Lord was thus disrupted for many years, but he continually burdened my heart and convicted me for turning away from Him. I ran away for 25 years but in 1998 He stopped me by allowing me to end up in prison for taking another man's life! Not only did He profoundly get my attention about the dead-end road I was on, but through GRM my eyes were opened regarding many aspects of false and misleading doctrine.

I am so grateful for this GRM course, Archbishop Dominique's and Rabbi Baruch's books and teachings, as well as my Messianic community. Through them and their teachings, I now know the whole truth about the Council of Nicaea and its Replacement Theology. I was aware of much of it, and I had already made an effort to repent and turn from it. However, this study and its in-depth yet concise teaching of Replacement Theology has opened my understanding to much greater levels of truth. The damage Satan perpetrated through Constantine at the Council of Nicaea by removing all things Jewish still curses the body of *Yeshua*, the Church, today. The realization of the truth of the millions of lives that have been lost because of the lies spoken by misguided, deceived church fathers such as St. Augustine and Martin Luther is astonishing! To this very day, those lies are still being taught. By His grace and direction, I hope to share the truth with many others, who will join us in true worship and praise through our Jewish Messiah! Just as Archbishop Dominiquae teaches, I believe it truly is a matter of life and death.

FINDING SHALOM IN THE OLIVE TREE

"I in them and You in Me—that they may be perfected in unity, so that the world may know that You sent Me and loved them as You loved Me."
— John 17:23

TESTIMONY OF J.L. (MALE)

GRM Bible School has impacted my life greatly, and I would like to share two ways that it has done so. First, the way I view myself as a believer has changed ever since I started this course. Through the book, *Grafted In*,* I have come to the knowledge that I am grafted into the Olive Tree of Israel and have become a partaker with the natural branches by faith in the Jewish Messiah (Romans 11:17). I now understand that the people of Israel are my brothers and sisters, so I stand with Israel! As it is written in Galatians 3:29, "And if ye be Christ's, then are ye Abraham's seed, and heirs according to the promise."

The topic that was most important and life-changing to me was women in the ministry. I have always believed in my heart that YAH can use anyone He wants for His purpose, even a woman in a leadership position in the body of Messiah, yet the scriptures were clearly against that, or so I thought! In his book, *The Woman Factor*,** Rabbi Baruch Bierman went through the Hebrew Holy Scriptures and showed how YAH had used women for His glory. He then delved into the original Greek meaning of the words in the New Testament to bring clarity to this topic. From the Hebrew Holy Scriptures to the New Testament Scriptures, many women had been used by YHVH: Rebecca, Deborah, Abigail, Hulda, Mary Magdalene,

---

* Available at www.ZionsGospel.com
** Available at www.ZionsGospel.com

Phebe, Priscilla, and the list goes on. After all, we see how YAH had used a donkey to warn Balaam (Numbers 22:28-30). If YAH used even an animal, why would He discriminate on the value of women in the ministry or leadership positions, since they are created in His image?

Secondly, my prayer life has changed. Dr. Dominiquae's course has imparted knowledge on the importance of praying for Israel in accordance with Genesis 12:3, "I will bless those that bless you, and I will curse him who curses you, and in you (Abram) all the families of the earth will be blessed." Now, I have included Israel in my daily prayers. I pray for Israel not only because of the blessings involved but because we are one through *Yeshua* by faith. The church and the Olive Tree of Israel were not meant to be separated but to be one (Romans 11:17). After all, it is *Yeshua*'s vision for oneness in John 17. I believe it is very important for the church to return to the Jewish Roots of their faith. Christendom, at large, has met a Roman Christ--not the true Jewish Messiah, and the fruit of that has been very destructive and divisive, creating much bloodshed and cruelty. I would like to thank Bishop Dr. Dominiquae Bierman for allowing the Ruach HaKodesh to use her in bringing this curriculum to fruition, which has been a blessing to me. I am now happy and at peace.

BACK TO THE ANCIENT PATHS

Thus says ADONAI: "Stand in the roads and look. Ask for the ancient paths—where the good way is—and walk in it. Then you will find rest for your souls.
 — JEREMIAH 6:16

TESTIMONY OF A.B. (MALE)

The GRM Israeli Bible School has allowed me the opportunity to study the Word of the Most High God and to call Him by His Name, YHVH. I have also learned the name of the Messiah, which means Yah (God) saves us — *Yeshua* (the Hebrew for Salvation). That salvation includes forgiveness of sins, healing of sickness, and deliverance from all oppression of the devil.

The 12 books that are a part of the GRM Bible School contain powerful messages that have changed my heart and the way I believe. I loved the journey of discovering and finding out the true identity of *Yeshua*, the Jewish Messiah.

I was able to study GRM Bible School at a fast work pace. I studied for hours each day and I couldn't wait for the lessons. This study took me to earlier centuries and opened up the truth of the Roman Catholic church in day-to-day language. I understood the general body of the congregation where I grew up in a new way. Hebrew was never talked about or preached, nor was Yah (God) called by His name. This program calls us back to the 'ancient paths' that Replacement Theology has long taught were dead. This was a labor of love and for love. Through the GRM curriculum, I also learned how to defeat the monster of antisemitism and be set free of its impact. The Church must return to its Jewish Roots, not to copy modern Judaism or pretend to be Jews, but to study Scripture, honor the commandments that have been forsaken, and become worshipers in spirit and truth.

FROM BROKENNESS TO A REPAIRER OF THE BREACH

"Some of you will rebuild the ancient ruins, will raise up the age-old foundations, will be called Repairer of the Breach, Restorer of Streets for Dwelling."

— Isaiah 58:12

TESTIMONY OF S.P. (FEMALE)

I grew up in a broken home where no one ever talked about God (YHVH) or Jesus (*Yeshua*). I was taken to a Catholic church only 4 times as a kid, so I did not learn about the Bible until I was 33 years old. A friend invited me to a Bible study and that was the first time I heard about Jesus Christ. I decided to receive Jesus Christ as my Lord and Savior, but I had a lot of questions that were left unanswered. I guess they did not know the answers because they never talked about the Jewish Roots, the Torah, or being grafted in. I began to learn about these things in prison in a Messianic class taught by the Chaplain.

It is really sad to know that the Jews were partially disconnected from their Jewish Roots. I am thankful that reclaiming the identity of the Messiah will lead to a worldwide enlightening revival ending antisemitism and that finally the Jewish People will be reconciled with their Messiah and with Gentile believers. Thanks to GRM Bible School for the history and knowledge that was shared with me, my eyes have been opened and my perspective has changed. Many of my questions have been answered. Now I will pass on what I have learned to others.

I FOUND SALVATION IN THE ONLY NAME POSSIBLE, YESHUA

For this reason God highly exalted Him and gave Him the name that is above every name, that at the name of Yeshua every knee should bow, in heaven and on the earth and under the earth, and every tongue profess that Yeshua the Messiah is Lord— to the glory of God the Father.

— PHILIPPIANS 2:9-11

TESTIMONY OF S.C. (FEMALE)

At first, I was a little hesitant about the course, but curiosity led me to it. I became interested in the Messianic practices not too long ago. However, due to the actions I observed by some of the women at Shabbat, I dropped the entire experience. Therefore, this study has been like a miracle for me, allowing me to view the Jewish roots of the Gospel in a new light. All the teachings have been eye-opening for me. I am amazed by the messages that are so clearly written. This teaching is a must for America, as our eyes have been blinded to the truth of our God.

I was raised as a Pentecostal believer, screaming at God, yet I have always been drawn to a different kind of relationship with God. In the GRM Bible School, I found what I was looking for. Realizing and understanding how Constantine changed the Gospel and spread a demonic lie to the world about our loving Savior, *Yeshua*, saddens me. I currently work in our chapel and thus have had the opportunity to read many of Archbishop Dominiquae's books. However, one of the most profound books for me is, *Yeshua is the Name.** I was raised in a very conservative Pentecostal home, and I was taught that there is no other name but the name Jesus. I was baptized at the age of 18 in the name of Jesus. To realize that my family and I had been deceived my entire life is very hard. Since I have had such strong opinions about the false teachings of the

---

* Available at www.ZionsGospel.com

Roman Catholic church, to realize I have been a part of that false teaching was incredibly difficult. Thank you for teaching the truth and allowing God to use you to bring salvation in the only name possible, *Yeshua*.

FINDING "HIS WAY"

So from now on we recognize no one according to the flesh. Even though we have known Messiah according to the flesh, yet now we no longer know Him this way. Therefore if anyone is in Messiah, he is a new creation. The old things have passed away; behold, all things have become new. Now all these things are from God, who reconciled us to Himself through Messiah and gave us the ministry of reconciliation.

— 2 Corinthians 5:16-18

TESTIMONY OF T.C (FEMALE)

I grew up being ashamed of my parents. My mother abused me physically and mentally, and my father was always working to support our large family of 6. As I grew, I rebelled more and more. We went to church with our mother but never stayed at one church longer than one year. Finally, as a teen, I turned my back on anything and everything my parents tried to enforce. I went through relationship after relationship, job after job, and lie after lie. Until this course, I never knew that all my rebellion was against the Bible, and I did not know the cause of my problems. I never fit in anywhere; I was always judgmental of others and never at peace. After learning about how Christianity has rejected Torah, I prayed to *Yeshua* and asked for forgiveness for all the wrongs I had done. After that, I slept better than I had in years!

A CLEANSED HEART AND OPEN EYES

"Moreover I will give you a new heart. I will put a new spirit within you. I will remove the stony heart from your flesh and give you a heart of flesh. I will put My Ruach within you. Then I will cause you to walk in My laws, so you will keep My rulings and do them."

— Ezekiel 37:26-27

TESTIMONY OF T.C (FEMALE)

Of all the books and teachings in the GRM Bible School, I think the book, *Grafted In*[*] stood out the most to me. This book has several chapters that changed the way I look at things. I will explain just a few. For example, the chapter titled, "Walk in My Holy Feast,"[***] dove deeper than anything I have read or been taught. The Spring Feasts: Passover, Unleavened Bread, First Fruits, and Shavuot all reveal the work of salvation! The Fall Feasts: Trumpets, Atonement, and Sukkot reveal the work of redemption! I am 46 years old and now I finally know the truth and will be able to explain things from a Messianic perspective, with knowledge, when I go home.

There is another chapter called, "Keep the Shabbat Holy"[****], which teaches that the weekly Shabbat is not a tradition... it's a commandment! Gentiles, such as myself, coming into the Covenant are required to honor YHVH's laws. In Yah's Eternal Kingdom, the Shabbat will be celebrated and honored by all nations. The concept of Shabbat was new to me until about three years ago. I grew up with Sunday being the day of rest, yet nowhere in the Scripture does it state that God changed the Shabbat to Sunday. Now knowing the truth, I cannot see Shabbat any other way than the way God wanted.

---

[*] Available at www.ZionsGospel.com
[**] Available at www.ZionsGospel.com
[***] Cite reference

I read and reread the book, *Grafted In*[*]. It taught me that to be grafted in is when Gentile believers allow themselves to become cultivated into the Olive Tree and nourished by its rich root. The strategy for the salvation of the world was, is, and will be the unity that happens when Gentiles join with the Jews in the same Kingdom, in the same Olive Tree. The grafted-in branch becomes one with the cultivated tree!

I now understand the Ten Commandments better and how to keep them. I begin and end each day in prayer and meditation in His Word, seek His face diligently, and keep my mind and mouth clean from worldly things. I will also get rid of anything that could be an idol when I get out and set up a home. I will keep the Shabbat holy and separate from every other day. I repented for dishonoring my parents and have forgiven many people and will continue to do so. I have repented of jealousy and will continually cleanse my heart and mind from sexual thoughts toward men and be more careful of how I dress. I will be honest in all my dealings and keep my word in all areas of my life. I will watch and wash my heart and remember that even "a little white lie" is still a lie, and thus a sin against God. I will keep myself busy doing the things of the Lord and be content with the things I have. I have also already changed my diet to follow the Levitical laws in Chapter 11, to eat kosher. I feel healthier and closer to God by eating clean.

This study has been a great eye-opener and a heart-cleansing experience. I have learned so many things that I was taught as truth, were lies. I will never look at the world's pagan-

---

[*] Available at www.ZionsGospel.com

influenced holidays the same again. I will only celebrate the feasts of the Lord and not let anyone make me feel ashamed. I can say that I never want to go back to the person I was before. I never want to go back to doing and believing lies. I pray to continue to show others what I have learned when I re-enter the world outside these gates and fences. I pray to find other believers to surround myself with! Most of all, I pray that one day I will somehow be able to visit Israel!

RECONCILIATION

My desire is to bless those who bless you, but whoever curses you I will curse, and in you all the families of the earth will be blessed.
— Genesis 12:3 (The Key of Abraham)

TESTIMONY OF S.M (MALE)

I was enlightened through the lesson "The Key of Abraham – Israel, our Mother" and the illustration that the church is born of Israel, and believers in Christ need to be reconciled once again to Israel. The same is true for my children and I. I believe that this ministry and my experiences in prison are helping me prepare for the blessings God will give to my family when we are reconciled from the sins of my past. I am guilty of provoking my kids to be angry at me and other adult figures in their lives. I pray the Lord will forgive them, for they know not what they do, and it was my fault, not theirs. The truths I have learned through GRM Bible School have changed me to be a better citizen in His Kingdom.

I AM NOT FORGOTTEN

"Can a woman forget her nursing baby or lack compassion for a child of her womb? Even if these forget, I will not forget you."

— Isaiah 49:15

TESTIMONY OF M.D.

Coming to the GRM Bible School is the best thing that's ever happened to me in my life. The love, support, and encouragement everyone on the GRM Team shows throughout this program is unbelievable. Just hearing the words, "I'm proud of you!" makes a big difference. The genuine love they have shown us in the prison shows us we're not forgotten. That means so much to me and all of us behind bars. I love and care about everyone who works at GRM because they have changed my life forever.

I learned from all the books included in the GRM Bible School the power *Yeshua* has if we just come to the Jewish Roots. GRM has greatly impacted my life because it has helped me see the light of *Yeshua* that we serve. I'm not saying that coming to *Yeshua* makes us perfect; we still make mistakes now and in the future. Dr. Dominiquae gives us an example of how, even with all the trauma and abuse that she encountered with her ex-husband, she forgave him and still loved him through all he put her through. This has helped me to forgive more people in prison for their disrespect. It's sometimes difficult to forgive someone, and it may take days or even years for someone to forgive another. The faith Dr. Dominiquae demonstrated in all her books has challenged me to go far beyond the faith I had before because I know without a doubt that if *Yeshua* can do it for Dr. Dominiquae, he can do it for me as well.

These books were the best books I've read in my life because of their honesty and authenticity. There's not one thing I disagree with in any of the books Dr. Dominiquae and her husband, Rabbi Baruch Bierman, wrote. They are 100% real and give it to you straight. GRM has helped me to stay focused on our Creator. I want to thank the GRM Team for the existence of the school. I can't even explain its profound impact on my life. Everyone who doesn't read these books is missing out on something amazing. They will teach you everything you need to know for a life-changing experience.

Dr. Dominiquae's salvation storybook, *YES!*,* was very sad. What her father went through was compelling, but in the end, he got to go home to *Yeshua*. *Yeshua* was with Dr. Dominiquae everywhere she went. She is changing the world through these books. I've learned to trust *Yeshua* more than I ever had before. Throughout this book, the lesson of obedience is emphasized. For example, once *Yeshua* told her to bring rice with her for the gathering, but she didn't, and it came out that a person who was supposed to bring it had forgotten all about it. She learned that when that "little voice" tells you to do something and you don't listen, you will regret it. It made me think about the times when *Yeshua* was trying to tell me not to do something, and I didn't listen to that voice, and I did wrong anyway, and now I'm in prison for 15 years. That 'still small voice' is the only voice inside you need to listen to. *Yeshua* only wants the best for us. No earthly father could ever love us the way *Yeshua* does. This book made me realize how important it is to listen

---

* Available at www.ZionsGospel.com

to what He tells me because it's only for my good.

Dr. Dominiquae's love for everyone and how she helps others is amazing. It inspires me to overcome my shyness. Talking in groups is difficult, let alone talking to someone one-on-one. I've struggled with that my whole life, and because of Dr. Dominiquae's example, I have given it to *Yeshua* by asking him to help me cast out the shyness. I need to come out of my comfort zone so I can help others the way she does.

GRM Bible School has changed my life forever. I want to give the whole team a shout-out and thank each of them. Thank you for all you do to reach out to all of us behind bars to remind us we are not forgotten! I encourage everyone reading this testimony to attend the GRM Bible school. It will be a life-changing experience for you.

A PLAN FOR SHALOM

"For I know the plans that I have in mind for you," declares ADONAI, "plans for shalom and not calamity—to give you a future and a hope."
 — JEREMIAH 29:11

TESTIMONY OF C.K. (MALE)

The Freedom from Pain Retreat* rekindled the fire in me to be the man Yah has called me to be. In my life, anger has caused me more pain than anything else. I have had to forgive being sexually abused by family and others. I also had to find a way to forgive my father for murdering my mother. The pain from that trauma alone made trusting anyone or having a genuine relationship, even with ADONAI, an almost impossible task. These are the things that hurt me most, as well as being incarcerated because of my own choices and thus separated from my wife, who is disabled and living alone. Ultimately, YHVH has shown me a love that has quelled my anger, allowing me to forgive those who hurt me and move forward. ADONAI has carried me through all the way. I know He has a plan for me; I am assured by faith it will come to pass, as it is written in Jeremiah 29:11.

What hurt me most in my life was that I blamed God for allowing my father to murder my mother, thus causing my siblings and me to suffer some very harmful and abusive situations as children. I felt that all of these things should have never occurred. However, YHVH has a purpose for everything, but we don't see the big picture until we come to Him. I have learned this in my walk through the teaching of the

---

* For more information about Freedom from Pain Retreat, write to info@grmbibleinstitute.com

Ruach HaKodesh, "...that all things work together for good for those who love God, who are called according to His purpose" (Romans 8:28, TLV). I have also understood that each day is a new and brighter walk down the path ADONAI directs me to walk. The Ruach has also taught me to "Trust in ADONAI with all (my) heart, lean not on (my) own understanding. In all (my) ways acknowledge Him, and He will make (my) paths straight" (Proverbs 3:5-6, TLV, my emphasis added).

As I have repented before ADONAI for ever having blamed Him for my mother's murder, learned to lean on YHVH, and have looked to the Scriptures to keep myself in line and on the right path, my pain has subsided, thus equipping me more to testify of His loving grace in my life and the freedom from the hurt and anguish I have suffered.

My love for ADONAI fills me with gratitude and awe. I am amazed at the "true calling" He has placed on my life. It humbles me to know Him and be known by Him. I trust in Him above everything in this world, and although I am incarcerated for life, I have been set free by his love and have thus dedicated this life to serving him to the fullest. I now know that he has always loved me. I am forgiven and living for eternity with Him.

Some of the most compelling Scriptures I look to keep myself on the straight path are in the book of Job, where it is written, "Yet He knows the way that I take; if He tested me I would come out as gold" (Job 23:10 TLV). Just as Job endured the hardship and loss of his situation, yet never cursed ADONAI, I too find myself able to say, "My foot has held closely to his steps; I have kept to His way and have not strayed" (Job 23:11 TLV).

NO MORE STARVATION

"If you give yourself to the hungry, and satisfy the desire of the afflicted, then your light will rise in darkness, and your gloom will be like midday. Then ADONAI will guide you continually, satisfy your soul in drought, and strengthen your bones. You will be like a watered garden, like a spring of water whose waters never fail. Some of you will rebuild the ancient ruins, will raise up the age-old foundations, will be called Repairer of the Breach, Restorer of Streets for Dwelling."

— Isaiah 58:10-12

TESTIMONY OF R.W.

The GRM Bible school taught me the fear and respect of Yah. I needed to hear that small, quiet voice. My studies with GRM have allowed me to develop a closer, more intimate relationship with *Yeshua* and the Ruach HaKodesh. I am now able to follow directions and guidance from spiritual sources rather than from the physical.

GRM Bible School was like a lifeline thrown from a boat to a drowning person. I may still be swimming, but I'm no longer in danger of drowning, and now I see the path to solid ground. This is not just another Bible school testimony; rather, it is a testimony of the Ruach HaKodesh gathering one more of the flock under His wing and using the GRM Bible school to do so.

Up to this point, my theological journey could be described as spiritual starvation. However, the solution to my spiritual malnourishment was always within reach; I just needed the right education to discern the truth. GRM Bible School has equipped me with the respect, fear, and knowledge I needed to foster a relationship with *Yeshua*. No more starvation!

I AM DELIVERED!

"A<small>DONAI</small> is my rock, my fortress and my deliverer.
— 2 S<small>AMUEL</small> 22:2

TESTIMONY OF R.C (MALE)

The deliverance program through GRM has been the most impactful and meaningful task I ever participated in. The preparation homework forced me to be honest with myself. I found things in my life that I compartmentalized as a child and built a wall of protection, thinking it was self-protection and self-preservation. I discovered all this was a lie and a prison the enemy had me in in my mind! I was honest with myself first by writing it out and getting it on paper. Writing these burdens down and reopening past wounds hurt more than I would like to admit, but it was very necessary for true healing!

After that, I put on my prayer shawl and sat under His wings; I felt now secure and safe. As Archbishop Dominiquae ministered to me through the audio recording of the deliverance session, I was led by the hand through the sweet tears of deliverance. I felt a mighty weight lifted off me and true peace like never before as I sat there with no weight on my shoulders and an overwhelming presence of peace. I began to ask God to fill me with His Spirit and fire, and I started speaking in tongues, which scared me at first, but then I realized it was the Spirit ministering to me. I am typing this essay with tears of thanksgiving; I can clearly and boldly proclaim that I am delivered!

DELIVERANCE FROM DARKNESS

For He rescued us from the domain of darkness, and transferred us to the kingdom of His beloved Son,
— **Colossians 1:13 NASB**

TESTIMONY OF E.P (MALE)

I'm not entirely sure what made me sign up for GRM Bible School. It may have been something to do because I'm confined to a cell or something deeper than I can ever imagine. I do know that I am forever grateful for being in the right place at the right time!

I used to be confused and uncomfortable because I didn't know what to believe. There are so many different doctrines, all going against each other and teaching different things. For years, I've been searching for the truth. And before, when I would seek, I would find things that were a bit unsettling. It made me turn away from it all and not care. GRM Bible School has done an extreme makeover in my life.

There were many times when I would pray for revelation, knowledge, truth, and understanding. GRM Bible School has given me that. Praise God! I now understand the Gospel better and know my faith's roots. I learned in another setting that knowledge in Hebrew means "light." So, the knowledge I've gained from GRM has shed light on the areas of darkness I had before.

Thanks to GRM, I have recommitted myself to God and truly accepted the Jewish Messiah. I'm no longer running around blind. I know the truth now, and nothing can change that! Bless Israel and the Jewish Messiah *Yeshua*! Praise God for deliverance from darkness!

NEW LIFE AND FAITH

Yeshua said to him, "I am the way, the truth, and the life! No one comes to the Father except through Me.

— John 14:6

TESTIMONY OF R.R (MALE)

The impact that the GRM Bible School has had in my life is that of breathing new life into a dying flame. I grew up in a religious household of the Christian faith where everyone went to church on Sundays and bible study on Wednesdays, but I've never really felt connected or that it was for me. I've been baptized and learned all the religious traditions. Still, deep inside, my faith was almost nonexistent because everything was forced upon me with a burn-in-hell scare tactic, while everyone preaching the messages and trying to influence my faith were hypocrites who participated in gossip and lived double lives outside of church and outside of Yah's Word. So, I ran from it all.

Being in prison, I've tried Islam and the Hebrew Israelites religion. However, in prison, people use religion as a social club for self-gain and even defile it by attempting to run it like a street gang that causes more corruption and destruction than anything. Thus, I did not want anything to do with religion and was giving up on having faith. Then someone introduced me to Judaism from the Jewish perspective over a year ago, but I was searching for answers on my own without the help of a rabbi until I came in contact with the GRM Bible School. Now, I have begun to receive real revelations and conviction of my sins when I'm doing wrong. My prayer life is gaining strength, and I'm more confident in my faith. I am aware of who Yah really is now and can recognize the voice of His Ruach HaKodesh. I am also seeing dreams, which I haven't been doing for many months. GRM Bible School has motivated me to grow in my faith.

YEARNING FOR THE JEWISH MESSIAH

"On the last and greatest day of the Feast, Yeshua stood up and cried out loudly, "If anyone is thirsty, let him come to Me and drink. Whoever believes in Me, as the Scripture says, 'out of his innermost being will flow rivers of living water.'"

— JOHN 7: 36-38

TESTIMONY OF J.S (MALE)

As a young child, my parents sent me to Bible school for vacation at 1st Baptist Church. I learned all the good stories in the Bible about Noah, Samson, David and Goliath, Jesus, and Christmas. That stopped after a while, but then my father got saved when I was 10 years old, and we all started going to Church every Sunday. I was indoctrinated into Replacement theology; we Christians were chosen while the Jews, the "Christ killers," were now the lost ones. Sunday was the new Sabbath, and we Christians were no longer under the law, which was for the Jews but not for us, the real chosen. We continued going to Church for approximately two years, and then we stopped.

So, for the next 35 years, I lived a life full of sin, always trying to fill the void in my heart. I never found what I was looking for until I came to prison. During my first week in prison, I found a Bible, picked it up, and never stopped reading. I read it from the beginning to the end. I was confused because what I read was not what I was taught as a child. I found that there is one Torah for both Gentile and Hebrew. I discovered that the Gentiles are grafted into Israel, and not the "Jews" grafted into the "church." I went to my Chaplain and requested a change of religion from Baptist to Kehilath HaDerek, the Messianic congregation. I met others who had the same understanding as myself. Now we have Erev Shabbat service, Tuesday night study, and Saturday afternoon service.

I have been looking for a Messianic Bible School for 9 years now! Thank you, oh so much! Your teachings are so informative from a Jewish perspective, not typical Christian theology. I learned much about the Covenants, the Ark of the Covenant, the Tabernacle of David, the Key to Abraham, and more. I also learned that I had been antisemitic in some of the beliefs that I had been taught. I also love your weekly Shabbat letters!* It helps me spread the truth of the Good News to the Orthodox Jews and the Christians.

---

* Sign up to receive our weekly mailings at www.kad-esh.org

FINDING THE HOLY SPIRIT

And this we will do, if God permits. For in the case of those who have once been enlightened and have tasted of the heavenly gift and have been made partakers of the Holy Spirit, and have tasted the good word of God and the powers of the age to come,
— Hebrews 6:3-5 (NASB '95)

TESTIMONY OF M.H (MALE)

After reading all the books and watching all the modules provided in the course, I felt my faith and conviction grow. As a Messianic Jew for 4 years who came out of Atheism, I was pretty surprised how, the year before I joined my congregation, I was severely misled by some Christian doctrine, specifically about the Holy Spirit. While I did learn the Torah, we never touched the subject of the Holy Spirit and its gifts. Due to that, I kept a misguided doctrine that the gifts of the Holy Spirit stopped when the last Apostle died. It did not help that many people claim they are led by the Holy Spirit here in prison. However, after the church service, they throw the Holy Spirit away and get high, fight, gamble, or do any other ungodly thing falsely prophesied. It was easier for me to hold on to the false doctrine I knew. But that changed as I did the GRM modules, especially when I studied about the Ark of the Covenant in level 3, wherein in the second episode, the Holy Spirit is upon Archbishop Dominiquae so that she weeps; it brought me to tears! I was entranced by this bible study. I am very impressed with how she teaches; there is no need for a smooth ear or pleasing words, just pure, simple truth. As a recently anointed elder of our congregation, I want to grow more in the truth and take my walk more seriously. All of us Elders in this prison congregation are taking the GRM Bible Study, and we recommend that our congregants study it also.

THE NUMBER 1

Yeshua said to them, "I am the bread of life. Whoever comes to Me will never be hungry, and whoever believes in Me will never be thirsty.
— John 6:35

TESTIMONY OF M.D (MALE)

This was the number one study I've completed; it has been life-changing for me. I gave my life to God as I was working on this course.

FROM CONFUSION TO CLARITY

Send forth Your light and Your truth— let them guide me. Let them bring me to Your holy mountain and to Your dwelling places.
— PSALM 43:3

TESTIMONY OF A.D (MALE)

For the past three years, I have dedicated my life to being a student of the Bible. I joined a Bible seminary and began a journey that led me to a master's degree in theology and completing all the coursework for a Doctorate. Along my journey, I encountered many inconsistencies with the Christian faith and vastly differing beliefs among the many church denominations. I became fascinated with these differences and wanted to understand why. You see, I grew up in Trinidad and Tobago, a small island in the Caribbean. The dominant church was the Catholic church, but the Pentecostal church was also quickly growing, and I attended both as a teenager. The Catholic church was all ceremony and repetitive prayer, while the Pentecostal church was the exact opposite, yet they both professed to believe in Jesus. Their doctrines also differed, which was very confusing. As an adult, I moved to the USA, where I encountered the Southern Baptist church and ultimately attended a Baptist Seminary.

A few months ago, I was talking to a friend who is a Messianic Jew about my struggle with my faith, and he introduced me to GRM Bible School. The first book I read was, of course, "The Identity Theft." This book really opened my eyes; it awoke something in me. The revelation that the faith I had devoted my life to had been divorced from its true Jewish roots clearly explained why there were so many inconsistencies in doctrine, why there was a lack of power in the Christian church, why no Christian church observed any of the feasts and why the "Old Covenant" was old and no longer relevant. Further study with GRM has revolutionized my understanding of Scripture and re-energized my faith, and I am excited to continue learning. I am truly thankful that I encountered GRM.

LEARNING TO KNOW MY FATHER IN HEAVEN

"...that the God of our Lord Yeshua the Messiah, our glorious Father, may give you spiritual wisdom and revelation in knowing Him."
— Ephesians 1:17

TESTIMONY OF J.E (MALE)

I've been in prison for 41 years. In all this time, I've done hundreds of bible studies, and I am sorry to say that none has inspired or fulfilled me as much as your course has. I've never felt as close to God as I do now. I feel I have a much better understanding of Him.

A whole new world has been opened to me. I want more of this study, as much as I can get. I've had so much bitterness in my life. Satan has had his way with me all my life, but I felt while I was reading and studying each lesson that Satan's hold on me wasn't as strong as it's been.

I'm finding myself talking more and more to God each day, asking Him to show me what He wants me to be, what His plan for me is, and what I can do to help carry that out. Thank you for giving me the opportunity to really know our Father in Heaven.

REMOVING THE BIGGEST STUMBLING BLOCK

I commend to you our sister Phoebe, who is a deacon in the church in Cenchrea. Welcome her in the Lord as one who is worthy of honor among God's people. Help her in whatever she needs, for she has been helpful to many, and especially to me.

— Romans 16:1-2 (NLT)

TESTIMONY OF W.M (MALE)

The module that meant the most to me was Women in Ministry. I was raised in a fundamental Baptist family. Pastors were always men; women could do secretarial work, cleaning and cooking for events, be Sunday School teachers for younger children or older girls, or, in the more "advanced" churches, possibly music directors. This was preached from the Bible, and at a very young age, I developed and maintained that women were always second to men. I remember my mother calling me a male chauvinist as a young teen, and I responded that I only believed what the Bible taught. As I got older, I grew slightly more lenient, even though when women were called Music Ministers, I would bristle, but for the most part, I went along, though if asked, I'd blame feminists and new age religion when the old ways were what was needed.

However, the people at the top of my list of the godliest/most spiritual people who had impacted my life were women. Still, I was very troubled in my spirit about so-called women pastors. I could almost wrap my head around women evangelists or guest/special speakers, but I still struggled with going so far as pastoring a flock.

Then I came to prison, and the Chaplain at the first camp I was at was a woman. She truly cared for her flock, and I could see that she was filled with the Spirit and fought for her inmates. I was at one of the toughest prisons in the United

States (rated #5 worst at one time), and yet, there was a presence of God at that chapel that was amazing. Some free-world people had to wait turns to come fellowship with us and said they felt more at Church with us than at their home church. I thought this woman Chaplain was an anomaly, and God must have made an exception because it was a prison.

I encountered more and more spirit-filled women and yet still blamed it on the prison exception, even though it did still bother me in my inner being. I thought it was slightly heretical because reading the Bible without knowing the context I now know; I struggled with wondering if I was being duped by false prophets or a wily Satan.

Then I heard about GRM Bible School and thought I'd give it a try. However, I rolled my eyes when it became evident that the leader was a woman. I thought she was mistaken in calling herself a bishop or a pastor, though I could feel the truth of Archbishop Dominiquae's teaching.

When her husband, Rabbi Baruch, started teaching a portion of women, I could immediately empathize with his experience (of opposing women in ministry in the past). The more I read and listened to him, the more I felt peace over this issue that I have struggled with for years! How often have I gotten things wrong by thinking the Bible was saying this when I never took the context into consideration?

To me, this should have been one of the easier teachings to accept, yet it was the one I struggled with the most. Finally, accepting this one opened my eyes to many other truths.

WHERE ARE YOU, GOD?

Guide me in Your truth, and teach me, for you are God, my salvation, for You I wait all day.
— Psalm 25:5

TESTIMONY OF Y.S.T (MALE)

I was 10 years old when I said YES to Jesus, to be not only my savior but my protector and my Lord. Not because one day I decided to go to church, but because I needed someone to take care of me and someone to vent my frustration about why, as a child, I had to go through everything I went through.

Forty years later, it was like I never gave my life to the Lord; it felt like the curse never was taken away from my shoulders. Many times, I asked God, where are You? Why do I have to go through all the hardship and misery even from my mother's womb (my relatives were waiting to adopt me, and my mom had to hide me)? And now I'm in prison; how is all this happening in my life; when will the curse in my life stop? I thought Jesus took all my curses away. Why is all this happening to me?

Eight years ago, after I had straightened up my relationship with God, I prayed that He would be the only one to open His Scriptures so I may truly know Him. Something apparently went wrong—the way I thought the Holy Spirit was teaching me was not the way of Christian teachings. I started to feel, believe, or say that something was wrong with Christianity, but I did not know what it was.

One day, my brothers in Christ asked me one of the weirdest questions I had ever heard: "Y., have you been talking with a Messianic believer or a Jew lately?" *What?* I rebuked them, ignoring the question. But now I realize the Holy Spirit itself was leading me.

Immediately after that, I transferred to another Institution, and the Holy Spirit led me to a Messianic Community meeting. They asked me, "Y., why do you have so much love for the Jewish people?" My reply was that they could give me some time to find answers to their questions.

Then, the GRM Bible course came as an answer to my prayers right on time. It explained everything to me, especially the reason why there was so much chaos in my life, even when I gave my life to the One who was supposed to protect me and guide me to all truth. I just found out that I have been believing a lie. Now I understand why none of the signs in Mark 16 followed us as believers and why there is so much hurt and brokenness within the body of Christ. Spirit of envy, murder, adultery, lies, anger, sexual immorality, etc., are in the churches all over the world because the Original Gospel made in Zion was replaced with a Roman gospel made in Rome.

Reading these anointed materials has made me cry as it has hurt me deeply to think of what we, the nations, had done against the people of Elohim God throughout the centuries. I have repented countless times, but yes, I felt for the very first time the hurting spirit of the Jewish people. Now, as a Grafted-in believer, I stand with the Jewish people; I cry with them, and I am hurt when they are hurt. Furthermore, now I understand and can truly pray for the peace of Jerusalem with meaning. Thank you to You, my Elohim God, and my mentor, Dr. Dominiquae Bierman.

I am committed to Elohim God and His people, Israel forever. I am an inmate in Florida, United States, and I will stay connected with this ministry to support them in prayer.

LOST IN RELIGION, FOUND IN MESSIAH

Therefore if anyone is in Messiah, he is a new creation. The old things have passed away; behold, all things have become new.
  — 2 Corinthians 5:17

TESTIMONY OF D.R (FEMALE)

GRM Bible School has given me YHVH. The God I had learned about growing up had always felt wrong. My mother was Catholic, and my father was Jewish, but he didn't practice it. I was raised Catholic, but all my friends were Jewish. I have always been fascinated with Judaism, but I didn't fully understand it. So, I was always kind of lost in religion. I have wanted to be a nun from as far back as I can remember. I have always loved God, even if I didn't understand Him. I just knew He was always with me and loved me. As I got into my 20s, worldly things got in the way. I looked at different New Age religions. Not having a solid foundation, I was easily swayed.

After coming to prison, I got deep into the Word. There were no more distractions. It was just me and *El Roi**. I was going to Christian services, and still, it just didn't feel right. Then I came across Rabbi Tony and his wife Diane, Messianic ministers, and my soul said, "Yes!" I knew everything had led up to me meeting them. I was where YHVH wanted me. Rabbi Tony connected me to GRM Bible school, which has saved my life! My physical life was dark, and my spiritual life was hanging by a thread because it was built on false doctrines and lies. I now have a deep, healthy, thriving relationship with *Yeshua*. My whole life has changed. The way I see, the things I hear, what I think - they are Messiah-like. I hear the Holy Spirit speak to

---

* "The God who sees me;" see Genesis 16:3

me, and I listen. I see El Roi in my daily life. I have countless blessings, and He has restored my family relationships. He has delivered me from my addiction and showed me my worth. I find great joy in keeping His appointed feasts, the Sabbath, and His Commandments. I have never had this wholeness, peace, and completeness. I have no fear in my heart as I walk on His Word and Promises. I am a daughter of the Most High God!

NO LONGER EMOTIONALLY CRIPPLED

Yes, and I ask you, true companion, to help these women—they labored side by side with me in spreading the Good News, together with Clement also and the rest of my fellow workers, whose names are in the Book of Life.

— PHILIPPIANS 4:3

TESTIMONY OF A.G (FEMALE)

GRM Bible School has impacted my life in such a way that I will never be the same! The Holy Scriptures have come alive, and my whole perspective on Torah has shifted to realize the importance of implementing Yah's laws, statutes, and ordinances to live in righteousness, holiness, and ultimately unbroken fellowship with YHVH Elohim.

Archbishop Dominiquae's teachings have helped me acquire a deeper understanding of the Scriptures and cultivate a much deeper relationship with *Yeshua* as my Savior, Healer, Redeemer, and Deliverer. I absolutely love speaking His true Hebrew name, knowing that it literally means salvation, healing, and redemption, and I share His true name with anyone who will listen.

He is making me know (yada) Him as my *Ishi*[*], and I can feel His Ruach HaKodesh living within me and moving through me in a mighty way.

I feel so free for the first time in my life because I now know my Messiah's true Jewish identity and what that means for me on a personal level. As a result, I now know my own true identity in Him!

The topic that was most important and life-changing for me was women in ministry.

---

[*] Husband in Hebrew

My mother was called into ministry and anointed to preach in the late 80's - early 90's, and I remember being a young girl of about four years old and older, listening to my mom preach in our little home church from a small podium that was placed on ground level with the pews of the congregation. I don't ever remember seeing my mom preach from the pulpit, which didn't occur to me to be an issue then as much as it does now. The church leaders said and did many other things to belittle my mother and quench the Ruach. Things that a young child couldn't fully comprehend. My father was the choir leader, deacon, and Sunday school teacher in our church, but I didn't see from him any of the support (to his wife as a minister) that was described in the last teaching of this course by Rabbi Bierman.

The church also had a skewed understanding of Paul's letters to the churches concerning women, and without the proper support from her husband and what should have been faithful friends, I witnessed my mother's persecution and falling away - not only from the church but gradually from the faith. We went to several churches after that but never found a church family, and the fear, discouragement, and bitterness that had successfully silenced my mother's ministry was passed on to me. I was to be seen and not heard, which greatly affected me on many levels. I've been spiritually and emotionally crippled by it for many years, but no longer, thanks to your GRM Bible School Courses!

I am now 36 years old and am stronger in my faith than I've ever been because I know the Truth, and it has set me free!

I have been completely liberated to disciple and teach anyone that God brings into my path with a strong message that Eve has been redeemed and is an equal to Adam and necessary in counterbalancing the work of the Kingdom. Though this is a new concept, I am determined to walk humbly in my God-given authority as a woman minister of the Gospel and hope to find a synagogue or church that is founded on the Jewish roots of the faith and will join God's mission to build His strong army of women.

My mother has suffered and is still suffering from what replacement theology has done to our churches, and I am in prayer that God will make a way for me to share with her, and many other silenced women, the Truth that GRM and Ruach HaKodesh has revealed to me.

ANOINTING IN THE DORM

I say then, God has not rejected His people, has He? May it never be! For I too am an Israelite, of the seed of Abraham, of the tribe of Benjamin. God has not rejected His people whom He knew beforehand. Or do you not know what the Scripture says about Elijah, how he pleads with God against Israel? "Adonai, they have killed your prophets, they have destroyed your altars; I alone am left, and they are seeking my life." ...

— **Romans 11:1**

TESTIMONY OF A.B (FEMALE)

This school has drastically impacted my life. I knew God had a purpose and plan for my life according to Jeremiah 29:11, but I couldn't figure out exactly what I was supposed to do. I was walking around in life, confused. When I came across this school, I felt so relieved. The Messiah opened my eyes. I immediately started repenting. I now understand how important it is to keep Shabbat and the Laws of the Messiah and be obedient. When I learned about the Council of Nicaea, the Spanish Inquisition, and the holocaust, I began to repent and ask the Messiah to forgive me for being ignorant about these. I started to become filled with the Holy Spirit and see the world through the Messiah's eyes, and immediately in the dorm, people were coming up to me asking me about Messiah and the GRM Bible School. The anointing spread in the dorm. I give ADONAI all the glory; taking this school has been the best decision I have ever made.

MY TRUE IDENTITY

For if you were believing Moses, you would believe Me—because he wrote about Me.
— John 5:46

TESTIMONY OF A.M (FEMALE)

Before my incarceration, I was being led to the Messianic believers after years of church trauma and wandering. I never fully understood the sickness of the root of it all, so going to a service with Archbishop Dominique and Rabbi Baruch here in prison was an amazing experience. I also found out that not only my Ukrainian side of the family was Jewish but also my Puerto Rican. It all made so much sense. I remember watching a movie years ago with my son called *The Boy in the Striped Pajamas*; it was a Holocaust movie. I was wailing at the end of it, and my son was saying, "MA, relax, it's just a movie..." and I lost it; I had a severe reaction to that movie – I screamed at him that it wasn't just a movie, this really happened to people! It took me days to recover from the deep heaviness in my heart. Now, it all made sense.

I remember asking church pastors, priests, and teachers so many questions about the Old Testament, and I was told not to read it, saying that Jesus took all that away. I believe they didn't know the answer, and I wasn't buying what they told me. Catholic upbringing had me Fear God the Father and not ask any questions to the other extreme of Crazy Christian doctrine: sin all you want; we got grace and the meek and lowly Jesus. I now know my identity, and I'm so in love with Israel and everything Jewish. I'm now on a mission to tell people everything I learned through this divinely ordained course.

FROM A GANG LEADER TO A PROUD MEMBER OF THE UNITED NATIONS FOR ISRAEL

For our struggle is not against flesh and blood, but against the rulers, against the powers, against the worldly forces of this darkness, and against the spiritual forces of wickedness in the heavenly places.
— Ephesians 6:12

TESTIMONY OF J.M. (MALE)

Eradicating the Cancer of Religion book* you gifted me opened my eyes to truly recognize that Muslim beliefs are nothing that belongs to YHVH. It put me on a journey that is not only transforming my life but also the lives of many I come in contact with. GRM Bible School is the best thing that has happened to me because it teaches me the real way!

Years ago, I was a very different person, very violent, but God has been working on me. I was second in command for a nationwide gang, and just recently, with the help of YHVH and GRM Bible School, I have begun to denounce that after 21 years of membership. However, they still acknowledge me, and I'm working on breaking away from that and them and enduring what I must to walk correctly for YHVH in *Yeshua*'s name. The enemy has been attacking me because of it. He knows he is losing a warrior, but I fight a different war for a different master now. I won't stop doing the course or moving in the right direction. I cry every time I see a message from you all. They mean so much. I know YHVH is involved because I never cry. I grew up rough and alone, and it made me cold and emotionless. But now I find myself crying so much it's like tears that have been missing for years, from all the deaths of my friends, adoptive parents, and mother of my first child to the loss of things, people, and love. Now, God's words bring

---

* Available at www.ZionsGospel.com

me to tears; your words bring me to tears, and certain sermons bring me to tears; it's how I know YHVH is actually in my life.

I am now a proud learning member of the United Nations for Israel, and I have had four other people read that book already, too.

Finally, thank you all; I love you all, and I love YHVH!

THE BLOOD OF THE FATHER GOD

For the life of the creature is in the blood, and I have given it to you on the altar to make atonement for your lives—for it is the blood that makes atonement because of the life.
— Leviticus 17:11

TESTIMONY OF R.D (MALE)

I read the *Eradicating the Cancer of Religion* book three times. The First time I couldn't truly understand what I had just read. The second time I was astounded, and the third time I understood what Archbishop Dominiquae was telling me.

From the time of Adam and the garden, His sole purpose was a personal relationship with a man. Satan came to the garden and, true to his nature, ruined man's relationship with God. All blood through Adam was sinful, and no amount of blood sacrifices could come close to removing that sin. God had to spill the first blood to cover Adam and Eve, and the only blood that could save us from the sin of Adam would be the blood of our Father God. So, God sent His Son, His blood, to die, save the world, and bring us back to Him. Religion had removed that personal relationship from God when all He wanted from us was oneness with Him and true love and devotion. I have been wrong all my life, but now I understand what God wants from me for the first time in my life! I cannot thank you, Rabbi and Dr. Bierman, enough for the gift you gave me, the gift of understanding and the true meaning of love. I pray that I never lose you from my life. I truly wish to continue my quest to have a relationship with God, as she explained in this book. Again, I thank you both for the gift of your love and the teaching to come.

END WORD

Saving the World

By Esther Yonah, MAP Prison Ministry Team Member

"I have not been in prison, but I have been locked in," I began our GRM Bible School service in a maximum-security prison. "I ended up in a mental hospital, and I spent over seven years in my private prison of sin, fear, anxiety, and fear. I was full of anger, bitterness, and unforgiveness. Finally, a friend gave me a book that you are now reading as part of GRM Bible School: The Healing Power of the Roots by Archbishop Dominiquae Bierman. As I started to repent of breaking the Father's commandments and found the original gospel with all its power and anointing from the pages of that book, I began to experience salvation, deliverance, and healing. I met *Yeshua*, whom I now know as my Jewish Messiah. However, I would have never guessed that I would find myself in an American prison…"

Often, when I share my testimony of being born-again-again in men's and women's prisons in Florida, I see many eyes in tears. After our Thanksgiving service, a huge, elderly man came to me weeping and said: I have been here for over 40 years, and this is the first time I hear *this* gospel! In a moment, we prayed together, and he received *Yeshua* as His Messiah. He felt truly unburdened for the first time in his life. We left hearts full of joy!

Truly, nothing is more rewarding than to see one more name written in the Lamb's Book of Life and witness the fruit of obedience and holiness in their lives. Deep restoration and healing have reached the impossible cases, and we give all glory to the God of Israel!

In his latest message, our student J.J. from a closed management dorm writes:

"I love the GRM teachings and can't get enough of watching the videos. There is so much stuff in there that I firmly believe people will benefit greatly from these videos. I wish they would show them at every church and every messianic Synagogue out there in the world."

How You Can Bless and Become Blessed by the MAP Prison Ministry

We invite you to pray for this life-changing ministry in the US prisons and support this labor of love. Your gift enables us to keep serving the incarcerated and providing them with our life-changing materials. You can donate at www.kad-esh.org (press on MAP Prison Ministry), or write to info@grmbibleinstitute.com to get more information of ways to give and support.

If you are incarcerated, we invite you to experience this same freedom others have received by studying GRM Bible School!

To enroll, send us a request by mail with your full name and corrections number, and we will help you to begin your studies.

Mail your inquiry to:

GRM Bible Institute
52 Tuscan Way, Ste 202-412,
St Augustine, FL 32092, USA

If you have incarcerated loved ones, we strongly suggest you share about the GRM Bible School with them. For more information and to inquire about the availability of GRM in a particular correctional facility, please write to info@grmbibleinstitute.com

Share the original gospel of Yeshua with your loved ones. A good start is to give them the Dr. Dominiquae Bierman's *Eradicating the Cancer of Religion* book, which will teach them how to find a relationship with the Living God of Israel through Yeshua, the Messiah. This book can be given to people from any religious or non-religious background. You can order it at www.ZionsGospel.com

If you are a prison staff member, we offer you a 50% discount on the GRM Bible School. We value and greatly appreciate what you do and want to give you this blessing that can equip you to continue your important work, filled with the Holy Spirit and Truth.

To request for Correctional Institution staff discount, please write to info@grmbibleinstitute.com

To invite our ministry team to introduce the MAP Prison Ministry, preach the Original Gospel made in Zion, and teach about Israel in your Church or Congregation[*], you can send your inquiry by email to info@grmbibleinstitute.com

---

[*] Mainly via Internet by Zoom

APPENDIX

Our Resources

Visit our websites and follow us on social media

United Nations for Israel

Take a stand for the restoration of Israel and transform your nation into a sheep nation, one person at a time. Become a member and join our monthly members' online conferences to get equipped!

www.UnitedNationsForIsrael.org
info@unitednationsforisrael.org

Israel Tours

Travel through Israel with our "Boots on the Ground" solidarity tours and take part in the prophetic restoration of Israel.

www.kad-esh.org/tours-and-events

Global Revival MAP (GRM) Israeli Bible Institute

Take the most comprehensive video Bible school online that focuses on the restoration of all things.

www.GRMBibleInstitute.com

info@grmbibleinstitute.com

Global Re-Education Initiative (GRI)
Against Anti-Semitism

Discover the Jewish Messiah and defeat religious Anti-Semitism! Order The Identity Theft and GRI Online Course Package

www.Against-Antisemitism.com

info@against-antisemitism.com

From Israel to the Nations TV Programs

Watch Archbishop Dominiquae Bierman's TV programs taped in the land of Israel

Roku Channel: Israel Revival

YouTube: Dominiquae Bierman TV

www.youtube.com/@DominiquaeBiermanTV

Rumble: Dominiquae Bierman TV

www.rumble.com/c/DominiquaeBiermanTV

MAP Prison Ministry

Through our prison ministry, pioneered by Rabbi Baruch Bierman, GRM Bible School is studied in prisons all over the USA. For more information & to support:

www.zionsgospel.com/map-prison-ministry/

Outlaw public display of Swastikas, Nazi, and Hamas flags

www.change.org/BanNeoNazism-Evil-Can-Be-Stopped

For more information about the founder of the ministries:

www.DominiquaeBierman.com

Books & Music

For more books by Dr. Dominiquae Bierman,
order online: www.ZionsGospel.com

The Israel Factor
Why October 7th Happened, Who Hamas Really is, and Why a Palestinian State is not a Solution but a Deception.

Truly Messianic
Become Anointed and Holy Spirit Empowered

Exposing Haman, Amalek, and Hamas
A Prophetic Secret of Purim for the Present Generation

The Voice of These Ashes
What are the Ashes of the Exterminated
Jewish People Crying For?

The Identity Theft
The Return of the 1st Century Messiah

"Yes!"
The Dramatic Life Story of an Israeli Woman who Falls and Rises Again Because of one Word: "YES!"

Restoring the Glory – Volume I: The Original Way
The Ancient Paths Rediscovered

The MAP Revolution (free E-book)
Exposing Theologies That Obstruct the Bride

Eradicating the Cancer of Religion
Hint: All People Have It!

The Healing Power of the Roots
It's a Matter of Life and Death!

Grafted In
It's Time to Return to Greatness

Sheep Nations
It's Time to Take the Nations

Yeshua is the Name
The Important Restoration of the True Name of the Messiah

The Key of Abraham
The Blessing or the Curse?

Stormy Weather
Judgment Has Begun and Revival is Knocking at the Doors

Restoration of Holy Giving
Releasing the True 1,000-Fold Blessing

The Bible Cure for Africa and the Nations
The Key to the Restoration of All of Africa

Vision Negev
The Awesome Restoration of the Sephardic Jews

Defeating Depression
This Book is a Kiss from Heaven

From Sickology to a Healthy Logic
The Product of 18 Years of Walking Through Psychiatric Hospitals

Addicts Turning to God
The Biblical Way to Handle Addicts & Addictions

Let's Get Healthy, Saints!
The Biblical Guide to Health

The Woman Factor by Rabbi Baruch Bierman with Dominiquae Bierman
Freedom from Womanophobia

The Spider That Survived Hurricane Irma (Free E-book)
God's Call for America to Repent

The Revival of the Third Day (Free E-book)
The Return to Yeshua the Jewish Messiah

Tribute to the Jew in You Music Book
Notes for the Tribute to the Jew in You Music Album

Music Albums
Abba Shebashamayim
Uru
Retorno
The Key of Abraham
Tribute to the Jew in You
Tribute to the Jew in You Instrumental

Teaching Series
God of Shalom
Israel in the War Series
The Powerful Women of the Bible

Support the Mission

Contact Us

GRM Bible Institute
www.grmbibleinstitute.com
info@grmbibleinstitute.com
52 Tuscan Way, Ste 202-412,
St Augustine, FL 32092, USA
+1-972-301-7087

Kad-Esh MAP Ministries
www.kad-esh.org | info@kad-esh.org

United Nations for Israel
www.unitednationsforisrael.org
info@unitednationsforisrael.org

www.ingramcontent.com/pod-product-compliance
Lightning Source LLC
Chambersburg PA
CBHW020856090426
42736CB00008B/401